CW00411309

The
BRIDGWATER
RAILWAY

by
J.D. Harrison

THE OAKWOOD PRESS

ISBN 0 85361 403 2

First Edition 1981
Second Expanded Edition 1990

Typeset by Gem Publishing Company, Brightwell, Wallingford, Oxfordshire.

Printed by Alpha Print, Witney, Oxon.

Acknowledgements

My thanks must be expressed to the following people for their help in providing drawings, photographs, sources and encouragement: Richard Dagger, Neil Pankhurst, John Childs, Chris Osment, Stuart Johnson, David Milton, Mike Palmer, Will Locke, Jonathan Edwards, Lens of Sutton, the Oxford Publishing Co., David & Charles, Robin Atthill, the late Norman Lockett, H.C. and Richard Casserley, Douglas Allan, Harold Tumilty, Jack Slinn, the H.M.R.S., the Somerset & Dorset Railway Trust, the Public Record Office, the House of Lords Record Office, David Bromwich, Dr A.J.G. Dickens, Harry Frost, Rod Fitzhugh, the National Railway Museum, Peter Cattermole, David Grimwood, Colin Maggs, J.E. Kite, Peter M. Ghie and Colin Judge. Thanks are due also to those that I may have unwittingly omitted from this list. Without the help and encouragement of so many people, research would be stunted and publication impossible.

Published by
The OAKWOOD PRESS
P.O.Box 122, Headington, Oxford.

Contents

The River Parret at Bridgwater as seen at the turn of the century.   *Oakwood Collection*

A publicity photograph taken on Cossington bank in the 1920s showing 4–4–0 No.70 pulling a bogie brake 3rd, two 6½ compartment bogies and a six-

SDRT Archive

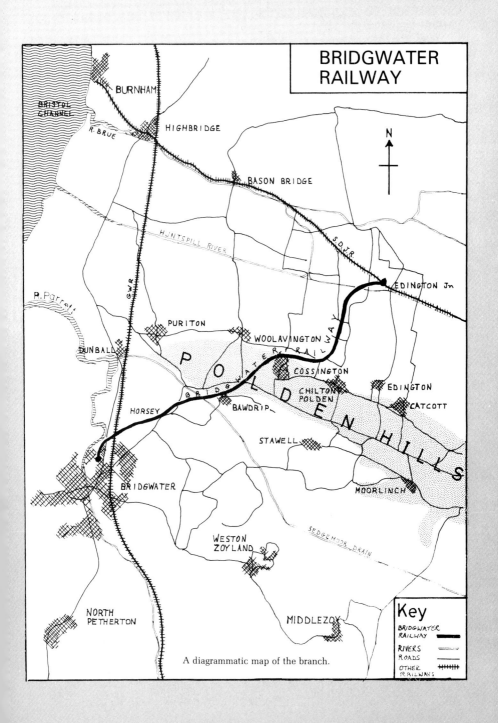

A diagrammatic map of the branch.

Introduction to First Edition

This book began several years ago when Will Locke, a fellow member of the Somerset and Dorset Circle, kindly showed me over the remains of the old Bridgwater Railway. His knowledge and deep affection for this line were immediately apparent. He knew the railway in his boyhood and later found employment on the line, where he met numerous railwaymen who had been involved with this local institution since its early days. A few years after Will's memorable guided tour he wrote to me stating that he thought that this 7-mile line ought to be the subject of a book, and asking me if I would help him to undertake such a task. At first I doubted if there would be sufficient material to warrant even a small book. A few visits to the British Rail archives before they were moved to Kew convinced me that there was at least a fascinating story that might make a magazine article or perhaps a short series in the Somerset and Dorset Bulletin, so I agreed to begin. However, like most mortals I have to earn a living, and had it not been for Will's prompting and enthusiasm this project would still be unfinished. Will agreed to write a chapter on his reminiscences, as I believed that he was far more able to describe the personalities of the line, and at the same time imbue this work with the love that he had for the railway. Furthermore he was part of the railway, whereas my experience of it was limited to riding on a bus underneath the Bristol Road bridge and once witnessing a train crossing the Sedgemoor Drain! Many of the operational details Will also supplied together with some of the photographs. Without Will's drive and enthusiasm this book would not have been written.

Why write the story of a relatively insignificant branch line that opened late and closed early? The story of the Bridgwater Railway is a fascinating tale that begins with the reasons for its construction in the first place. This intriguing beginning then leads one on to ask further questions about the line's rise and fall, its personalities, its place in the community, and reasons for closure. The creation of a small railway line and its subsequent life and death differs little from the histories of great civilisations, kingdoms, governments or peoples. They are shaped by the actions of men, based on thoughts and motives limited by environment, finance and morals, all of which respond to changing circumstances in time. This is the stuff of History. Hopefully, this little history reflects those ingredients.

J.D. Harrison

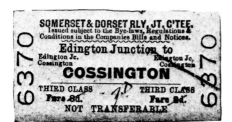

Introduction to Second Edition

To co-incide with the centenary of the opening of the Bridgwater Railway, the committee of the Somerset & Dorset Railway Trust considered that along with the appropriate celebrations there ought to be a second edition of *The Bridgwater Branch* published. To protest that I had enough to do and that anyway there was not really anything to add to what had already been written did not carry any weight. When Neil Pankhurst unearthed the contractor's drawings for the line and offered to redraw them and Colin Judge gave me free rein to rewrite and include more pictorial material, then to protest further would have been churlish. Thus the opportunity has been taken to add new material that has come to light recently and to rewrite several chapters. If just a few people find some pleasure in browsing through this small book then the effort will have been worth while.

1990   *J.D. Harrison*

Cossington Station, complete with all the furnishings of an S&DJ branch: ground-frame hut, electric telegraph board, timetables, billboards, firebuckets, benches, canopy, barrow and nameboard.   *Lens of Sutton*

Driver George Yard and Fireman Norman Cook crew No. 43218 (ex-SDJR No.73) on a mixed train at Cossington in 1951.

N. Lockett, Robin Atthill Collection, SDRT Archive

Chapter One
Prelude

At 11.30 am on 1st June, 1841, the Band of the West Somerset Yeomanry stirred the minds of the people of Bridgwater and welcomed the Iron Horse to this important Somerset town. The engine *Fireball* and its train of eight carriages heralded a new transport era that was to affect everyone in the town. Fast and reasonably cheap travel everyone could immediately appreciate,but the greatest impact was on trade. If the prices of goods in the shops did not go down there was certainly a greater variety of goods and profits probably increased. A host of new destinations and markets for Bridgwater's merchants enabled them to look forward to a period of prosperity.

A glance at Emmanual Bowen's map of Somerset c.1760 quickly reveals Bridgwater's importance as a centre of trade and transport before the Railway Age. This mediaeval town is the lowest crossing point on the River Parrett with roads radiating to Axbridge, Bristol, Bath, Wells, Glastonbury, Langport, Somerton, Taunton, Watchet and beyond. Small vessels plied regularly for hundreds of years across the Bristol Channel, around the South Western peninsula and across to Ireland. In mediaeval times Bridgwater boats took pilgrims *en route* to the shrine of Santiago de Compostella. By the 19th century emigrants could embark at Bridgwater for the New World.

Inland navigation was late in arriving at Bridgwater. In 1827 the Bridgwater & Taunton Canal was completed from Taunton to Somerset Bridge where it joined the River Parrett. In 1841 the canal was extended to join the newly constructed Bridgwater docks. This was the canal's last gasp as it was unable to compete with the new Bristol & Exeter Railway.

As neither roads nor canals could effectively compete with the B & ER, the railway company had a virtual monopoly of Bridgwater's transport and thus controlled its trade. The importance of this was not lost on several Bridgwater merchants whose interests were usually represented by the Corporation which had been used to controlling trade for hundreds of years. They had not been slow to put obstacles in the way of the Somerset Central Railway's plans to develop Highbridge and Burnham as rival ports in the 1850s. In 1865 they petitioned the B & ER in taking over the canal and docks to improve the latter. This the B & ER complied with, but now armed with such a comprehensive monopoly, they were free to determine not only rates but also the merchants who wished to rent warehouses and other facilities in the docks. Those on whom the B & ER bestowed favours were content. Most of the others merely grumbled while some waited in hope of breaking the monopoly. In the meantime everyone had to live with the B & ER and trust that the railway would meet their requirements. Each time that the B & ER system faltered, criticism of their efficiency and monopoly was raised. Competition, it was believed by many, would bring lower rates and greater efficiency.

There was no imminent danger of competition for the B & ER in the 1840s and 1850s. This was a time of expansion. As a broad gauge company the B & ER had access to London over the Great Western Railway. By encouraging feeder lines it could increase its own trade with the metropolis and expand its own territory at the expense of the narrow gauge companies in the South. The Gauge Act of 1846 by limiting the broad gauge to the GWR and its allies' territory had spelt the beginning of the end for the broad gauge. Thus the broad gauge companies jealously defended their territory. However, by 1862 one of the B & ER feeders had transferred its allegiance to the narrow gauge camp. This was the Somerset Central Railway, opened in 1854, thanks to B & ER backing, between Highbridge and Glastonbury. Although the SCR owned its line, it leased it to the B & ER who agreed to operate it and pay a guaranteed dividend of 4 per cent. Actually Bridgwater had been considered as the western terminus of this line but the heavy cost of crossing the Polden Hills and the recommendation of an Admiralty survey that Highbridge was suitable for development as a packet port postponed the link with Bridgwater. By July 1855 the SCR had obtained powers to extend their line to Wells and Burnham. A year later authority was obtained for an extension to Bruton to make a junction with the Wilts, Somerset and Weymouth Railway and meet the narrow gauge Dorset Central Railway. By 1862 the Somerset Central had laid narrow gauge track and amalgamated with the Dorset Central to form the Somerset and Dorset Railway, a line connecting the Bristol and English Channels. Independence was gained by ending the B & ER lease, the purchase of rolling stock and the recruitment of operating staff.

Once the optimistic euphoria died away, the S & DR found that the cost of independence was high. It had a channel-to-channel route, it was able to import coal and iron at Highbridge and export agricultural produce. Unfortunately this was not enough. The line served no large centre of population. To pay its way it had to seek greater traffic. The agricultural South did not offer much prospect but the industrial North could generate the size of traffic that a railway manager's dreams are made of.

One major problem was the break of gauge at Highbridge. The S & DR was dependent upon the co-operation of the B & ER in carrying northbound traffic out of Highbridge. It had been hoped that the B & ER would have laid narrow gauge track between Highbridge and Bristol, but they had not and were in no hurry to do so. Thus the S & D planned a line from Wells to Yatton hoping to get running powers over the B & ER to Bristol. The latter blocked this plan by proposing a line from Uphill to Wells. Meanwhile a line was mooted from Evercreech to the Bristol and North Somerset line at Radstock. This was to be worked by the S & D and owned jointly with the B & NSR. The day before the Bill was to be presented to Parliament the B & NSR announced that they had entered into an agreement with the GWR whereby the Great Western would operate the B & NSR and that the proposed link with the S & D was to be dropped. It was in this sort of atmosphere that the S & DR's first serious attempt to enter Bridgwater was foiled.

In November 1865 the B & ER became aware of an S & D plan to build a line from Shapwick to Bridgwater. Actually it was the 'town of Bridgwater' which promoted the Bill. The S & DR was in severe financial straits and unable to subscribe to the capital of the undertaking, but agreed to work the line for 40 per cent of the gross receipts and if the remaining 60 per cent did not yield 5 per cent profit then the S&D would give a rebate sufficient to achieve 5 per cent. Using hindsight such an undertaking seems absurdly optimistic. Perhaps it was an attempt to attract subscribers, trusting that once the line was built traffic would grow sufficiently to enable them to pay 5 per cent. Anyway, this Bill was thrown out by the Commons Committee when the B&ER presented a competing Bill in which they promised to remove all the complaints that the Bridgwater people had. Bridgwater Corporation had sent the B&ER two memorandums in 1865 which expressed hopes that the railway company in taking over the Canal would improve the docks at Bridgwater, build an extension of their line to the docks and to a cattle market shortly to be built nearby and finally to lay down narrow gauge track between Yeovil and Bridgwater.

Having satisfied Bridgwater's wishes in their Bill, it was not surprising that the Shapwick-Bridgwater line was thrown out. After all, Bridgwater would now have its docks improved and be given access to the narrow gauge system at Yeovil. However, the Commons Committee insisted on the incorporation of two facility clauses (Nos. 46 & 47) whereby the narrow gauge line was to be laid between Yeovil and Highbridge within two years and that satisfactory arrangements had to be made to provide for traffic to and from the S&D system at Highbridge. J.C. Wall, General Manager of the B&ER recalled that he was directed to make such arrangements as would completely satisfy the directions of the Committee. He added that there had been a great deal of correspondence between R.A. Read, Secretary of the S&DR, and himself and that the B&ER incurred very great and very frequently unnecessary expense in putting on trains at inconvenient hours to meet S&DR traffic at Highbridge, because he did not want to incur the penalty clauses as it might tell against the B&ER in the future.

The defeat of the Bridgwater-Shapwick line had cost the B&ER dearly. Laying the narrow gauge between Highbridge and Yeovil accounted for £40,000 while another £120,000 was spent on improving the old horse tramway from the B&ER line to the Parrett, purchasing property, putting in sidings, erecting steam cranes, building the telescopic bridge and laying track around the docks. On the other hand it was a long term investment for the B&ER. They knew that the days of the broad gauge were numbered and that they would have to lay narrow gauge one day anyway. Furthermore by acquiring the docks they would encourage traffic growth and enjoy a monopoly.

So. West. and Mid. Railway Companies'

Som. and Dor. Joint Line.

TO

BRIDGWATER (S. & D.)

Vulcan 0–4–4T No.52 was allocated to Bridgwater for a time.
L&GRP Collection, courtesy David & Charles

Another Bridgwater based 0–4–4T, this time Avonside No.32 photographed alongside the departure platform at Bridgwater in 1905. *L&GRP Collection, courtesy David & Charles*

Chapter Two
Campaign of 1875: Bridgwater's case

If the B&ER had been able to satisfy its Bridgwater customers, if the S&DR had been sobered by its financial failure, if there had not been so much ill feeling between broad and narrow gauge interests, then the attempts to drive the S&DR into Bridgwater would have ended in 1866. In that year the S&DR went to the Court of Chancery. Four years later the Receivers were discharged and the S&DR picked up from where it left off, penetrating northwards into the Somerset coalfield and looking for a narrow gauge outlet to the north. The resultant Bath Extension.opened in July 1874,posed a severe threat to the B&ER. Here was a narrow gauge line from Poole, with a junction with the LSWR at Templecombe and an outlet to the Midland at Bath. The B&ER was in competition with the LSWR at Exeter and Yeovil, and at Bristol it had the disadvantage in its dealings with the Midland of a break of gauge thus giving the S&DR an important advantage in north-south traffic. The fact that the latter was once more in a sorry financial state increased the B&ER's worries in case the S&DR should seek absorption by the Midland Railway, thus hitting the B&ER's lucrative northern traffic.

At the same time, discontent with the Bristol & Exeter resulted in another attempt to promote a line 7 miles 3 furlongs from Edington on the S&DR terminating in 'Bridgwater, in a garden on the west side of the road called Church St.' and a further 5 furlongs, 2 chains and 11 yards to the right bank of the Parrett. The promoters of the Bridgwater Railway were keen to point out that their's was an independent railway. Robert Arthur Read, General Manager of the S&DR emphasised that there was no financial connection between itself and the Bridgwater Railway. Few people were fooled by this, least of all the B&ER Engineer, Francis Fox, who stated,

> When I see the solicitor of the Somerset and Dorset Railway Company promoting the Bill, and when I see Mr Read, the well-known General Manager of the Somerset & Dorset Railway, here supporting it, and when I find that they are going to work it, I think that very few persons connected with railway matters can have much doubt as to what was the intention.

This nominally independent company had been set up by those who controlled the destiny of the impecunious S&DR to expand their territory while dispersing their financial liabilities. How a near bankrupt company can expand may seem puzzling, but Francis Fox was not surprised.

> I have such confidence in Mr Read's extraordinary talent in financing that I have no doubt, after they get their Bill, they will do as wise people should do, call in Mr Read, and by some process, which I am ignorant of, obtain the money.

This railway could not have been promoted if the people of Bridgwater had been content with the B&ER. A public meeting revealed how popular the proposed line to Edington was. Out of 4,000 or 5,000 present only four opposed the proposal and two of the opponents were pressing for a line to Glastonbury via Chedzoy, Mallets, Moorlinch, Ashcott, Walton and Street. The promoters of the Bridgwater Railway were able to summon support from many influential people in Bridgwater, all of whom had some criticism to make of the B&ER.

Train services were attacked by Joseph Smith, alderman, mayor three times, magistrate and guardian of the poor. He complained that he could not get to London before 2.35 by the B&ER/GWR. If he drove to Highbridge he could, via the S&D/LSWR reach Waterloo by 2.05. Furthermore the B&ER only ran one third class train in each direction while the B&E trains that were supposed to connect with S&D services were late nine times out of ten. Even allowing for Mr Smith's exaggeration there appeared to be some substance in his case.

On the freight side the complaints were even louder. Charles Bailey, Director of the West of England Oil Cake Co. who sent most of their produce into Hampshire and Wiltshire via the LSWR, stated that when he instructed that goods for Bournemouth should go over the S&D, the B&ER sent them over its own route via Yeovil at an 'exorbitant price'. Bailey's chief complaint was about the lack of narrow gauge trucks,

> . . . even before this line was laid out at the dock . . . the cake was carted about by J.C. Wall's wagons . . . our cake got mixed upon the dock . . . some got overweight and some . . . shortweight, and since the loopline has been cut to the docks . . . I have had to wait 6 or 7 days before we could get a supply of narrow gauge trucks . . . it takes three days before (trucks are) cleared from Bridgwater station . . . many of our customers . . . are very often kept waiting a fortnight or three weeks . . . on account of the constant delay occasioned by the B&ER.

Gilbert Simmonds, town councillor and manager of Colthurst Simmonds & Co., brick and tile manufacturers had a similar complaint as also did James W. Sully, principal proprietor of Park End Colliery Co. in the Forest of Dean, shipowner and coal merchant in Bridgwater. Many thought that Sully was favoured by the B&ER, but his need for trucks led him to persuade the latter to order another 200 wagons. Sully owned a number of his own wagons but he felt that private owners wagons were a poor investment,

> I have so much as 90 or 100 trucks of my own, and I have laid out £10,000 and cannot get any interest for the investment; they only allow me 1/8th of a penny per ton per mile for the maintenance of the trucks, and it does not pay the maintenance.

It was the B&ER monopoly that upset many of Bridgwater's merchants. John Hammill, JP, guardian of the poor, commissioner of pilotage, former mayor, timber shipper, general exporter and manufacturer of bricks and tiles pointed out that many small shipowners were unhappy about 'trade getting into the hands of a few connected with the B&ER'. John Soper, grocer and town councillor, revealed that James W. Sully was a Director of the B&ER and has 'pretty nearly exclusive use of the dock'. Alfred Peace, general corn, hay and potato merchant, S&D agent at Shepton Mallet, Pickford's agent, shipping agent and furniture van proprietor, stated that as managing owner of a line of steamers between Liverpool and Bridgwater he was not allowed to get ground for a shed in the docks thus he had to discharge goods upon the open ground and eventually to take off the steamers altogether.

In supporting the Bill the S&DR showed how ineffectual were the clauses 46 & 47 inserted in the B&ER's 1866 Bill to facilitate traffic between Bridgwater and the S&D. Although those clauses stipulated penalties if they were not complied with, R.A. Read pointed out that approaches could have been made weekly to the Board of Trade. The B&ER,

> ... having the entire control as to their own railway and their own station at Bridgwater and so on, they are in a position to obstruct, and certainly would not naturally facilitate another company's competition for the Bridgwater traffic, and I think it is very natural that they would not be desirous of giving facilities; they are in a position to throw obstacles in the way, and a great variety of those obstacles might be occurring every day, or every week.

As an example of the B&ER breaking with the spirit of the facility clauses, Read reported that he had asked that company to get one narrow gauge train a day altered to a later departure from Highbridge so that goods traffic had time to arrive from Salisbury or London. The B&ER did not acquiesce. To add weight to their argument about the uselessness of the facility clauses, Robert Underdown, General Manager of the Manchester, Sheffield and Lincolnshire Railway stated,

> I told the S&D company that they had got something worse than nothing when they got those clauses.

He went on to explain that even if the Board of Trade or the Railway Commissioners enforced a through rate, the traffic in Bridgwater was in the hands of the B&ER who had no interest in encouraging such traffic. Simply, the case was that while the B&ER controlled traffic in Bridgwater it was not in their interest to encourage trade for a rival company.

Those then were the chief grumbles about the B&ER. Add to them the disadvantages of the need to change goods from broad gauge trucks to narrow gauge, complaints about lack of civility and the general desire for better communication with the LSWR system and we have a formidable case for the Bridgwater Railway.

There had been a chance that the B&ER would not oppose the Bill. They offered to drop their opposition if Toogood, the S&D solicitor dropped his opposition to a B&ER Bill. Presumably Toogood would not co-operate so the Bristol & Exeter vigorously opposed the Bridgwater Bill and rallied support in the district to be served by the line.

Thomas Ware, corn merchant in Bridgwater and Highbridge and a tenant of the B&ER revealed that he imported mostly oats from Ireland, the Baltic and Prince Edward Island and that he regularly sent these imports to Basingstoke, Salisbury, Southampton, Devizes, Evercreech, Exeter and Plymouth. Seven times out of ten he claimed that the B&ER would quote a cheaper rate than the S&D. Ware saw no advantage in the Bridgwater Railway as ships discharging at its wharf would have to lie on the river bank. He would not allow ships carrying cargoes valued at £4,000 or £5,000 to lie anywhere but in a floating dock such as the B&ER possessed.

On the question of shortage of trucks, William Holland, a partner of Brown & Co., Bath brick manufacturers, had no difficulty in obtaining S&D trucks in Bridgwater. J.C. Wall admitted that there could be a shortage of trucks for furniture vans but that this only really occurred at quarter days and because of the exceptionally large size of these vans. J.W. Sully added that when he considered opening a branch business at Highbridge the S & D was unable to provide trucks or plant and that this together with the fact that Highbridge did not have a floating harbour deterred him from opening his branch.

The Bridgwater desire for competition was ably dealt with by J.C. Wall. Competition, he said, would not bring rates down. He cited the attitude of Scott of the LSWR when they reached Exeter. Scott thought that the B & ER rates were too low so that company's rates were brought up to LSWR rates. According to Wall, 'Competition always ends, as far as railways are concerned, in combination'. Wall was basically correct as far as rates and fares were concerned. A parliamentary enquiry in 1872 had concluded that there was no active competition in monetary matters.

Competition in facilities, accommodation and parliamentary committees still existed. The B & ER were quick to compete in this area by pointing out that the distance between Bridgwater, Highbridge and Templecombe on the one hand and Bridgwater, Durston and Yeovil on the other differed by only 1½ miles. They were also able to back a landowner, Mr Broderip, in his opposition to the line cutting across his property in Bawdrip. It was claimed that a cutting could be seen from Mr Broderip's house. R.J. Ward, the Bridgwater line's Engineer, was very surprised by this as he had taken pains to accommodate Mr Broderip's apprehensions about the railway. William Eve, the Bridgwater line surveyor noted that the B & ER had shown the line on its plan to be much closer to Mr Broderip's house than it would be. To counter Mr Broderip's opposition the Bridgwater company produced the rector of Bawdrip and the vicar of Woolavington and Puriton to talk of the advantages of the line to their parishioners and the cattle drovers.

On 17th March, 1875 the Commons Committee decided that the Bridgwater Railway had proved its Bill, but asked that they obviate Mr Broderip's not unreasonable objections. The next step was to seek the approval of the House of Lords. As the B & ER was unlikely to produce anything of consequence to stop the Bill in the Lords this step should have been a formality, the line would get its Act and within a few years Somerset & Dorset trains would be seen in Bridgwater.

Fowler, No.23, on the departure road at the north end of the island platform at Bridgwater in 1928. In the left background can be seen the water tower and part of the roof of the coaling-stage.   J.E. Kite

Chapter Three
Campaign of 1875: Bribery and Corruption

The Bill did not reach the House of Lords. It has been assumed that either the promoters felt that they could not raise the capital or that the B&ER managed in the interim to stack so much opposition that it was not considered worthwhile pursuing the project. That the B&ER determined to oppose the Bill in the Lords is certain. Then in June 1875 the B&ER minutes revealed that Toogood was paid £2,000 on the withdrawal of the Bridgwater bill and a memorandum was sent as to the payment of an additional £1,500. So that was it, the B&ER and the Bridgwater Railway had come to an amicable agreement. Or was the agreement with the S&DR, as Toogood was solicitor to both? That was odd; surely the minutes would have recorded the payment to the company concerned rather than the name of an individual?

The truth behind the end of the 1875 Bill emerged seven years later when another attempt was made to gain Parliamentary approval. The beans were spilt by the GWR's carting agent for the West of England, the same man who until its take-over by the GWR had been General Manager of the B&ER, none other than James Cresswell Wall. His revelation is worth reporting:

> I met Mr Toogood after the passing of the 1875 Bill and I jokingly said, 'Now you know, my friend, this line is not wanted, it cannot be any use to anybody, and I can understand that your principal object was a sort of commercial speculation. Now do you really want it?' He said, 'Oh yes, we want it certainly'. I said, 'We shall oppose it in the House', and I said, 'The best thing would have been for you to consider whether the money we spend in opposing this Bill in the House with success, will not be much better in your pocket. We do not care about the Bill, if you turn it over in your mind and let me know, we will see if an arrangement can be made'.
>
> A day or two afterwards I met Mr Toogood and he said 'I have thought about the matter, and provided we can come to terms I do not care about going on with the Bill'.
>
> We did come to terms, the money was paid, and the Bill went no further.

This revelation caused a great deal of consternation and embarrassment, but more was to come. Wall revealed that Toogood was paid to drop the Bill entirely on his own account and not as solicitor for the promoters. One sum was for his expenses because the S&D was impecunious and another for his profit because he said, 'No, I cannot be without profit'. Toogood had said that he was disappointed with the subscription and that practically it fell upon his own shoulders.

Wall stated he had not come to boast about the matter, but had spoken out as the Bridgwater counsel had given the impression that the B&ER had bought the Bill so that they could make the line themselves. He added that the Bill had been, 'a speculation like other such matters, and if I could get rid of it properly, and with the consent of the promoters, I would suggest it to my Directors and that was done.'

Toogood was present while Wall was making the Bridgwater party squirm. His counsel refused to call him, saying that he would not go into personal matters before their lordships! Naturally he was instructed to deny the whole matter. Wall came right back by suggesting that Charles Pritchard, the Bristol solicitor for the B&ER could corroborate his story. Pritchard was called and agreed that Wall's story was correct. Pritchard had been content to deal with Toogood alone and pay him the money because 'he had the whole control of the Bill.'

Wall had thrown mud and Toogood, unable to duck, was plastered. That he survived this besmirchment of his character and continued as solicitor for the Bridgwater Railway makes one wonder how much of the mud stuck to the others involved, not only in promoting the line, but also those associated with him in the S&D. What appears to be a case of straightforward bribery at the expense of those who were genuinely wishing for a line between the S&D and Bridgwater seems to have been condoned by his associates. How much mud adhered to the officers and Directors of the S&D? Apart from the fact that his services were not dispensed with there is no evidence to show that others were directly involved.

We can feel sorry for Toogood for being exposed publicly, for having risked his own money with little prospect of getting it back and for being in a position where he was apparently left holding the baby. Nevertheless, there are certain questions that need to be asked. Firstly, Wall made it very clear that the B&ER regarded the line as a speculation that few people wanted. The fact that the subscription was disappointing tends to back that up. Who then was the speculator? Was it Toogood alone? How deeply was Read involved or was he being used by Toogood? How much was the S&D Board involved? That they could not render direct financial assistance suggests that they were not the speculators, but they were certainly used as the vehicle for penetrating B&ER territory in Bridgwater. A speculation involves risk, but Toogood was a solicitor specialising in railways and surely he was too intelligent to risk his own money? The chances of a return from investment in the Bridgwater Railway must have been remote. The S&D had paid no interest worth mentioning since it became independent. Toogood was too clever a man to invest on hopes. Perhaps his motives lay elsewhere. Drive a line into B&ER territory; whether it pays or not is irrelevant. You then offer your line either to the B&ER or one of its rivals, whoever will pay you the fattest guaranteed dividend. The rival will be eager to expand its territory while the B&ER will be eager to defend its territory.

It is interesting to note that the speculation got as far as it did. One reason was that there was considerable support in Bridgwater especially among the merchants. Without their discontent with the B&ER and their vocal support the line would have been very difficult to promote. However, when it came to digging into their pockets they were not so forthcoming. Nevertheless, a sympathy and a desire for the Bridgwater Railway remained and in 1882 it was exploited again.

Chapter Four
Campaign of 1882

The dropping of the 1875 Bill had caused great chagrin in Bridgwater. Before another attempt was made to build the Bridgwater Railway, two major events occurred. In November 1875 the Somerset & Dorset was jointly leased by the Midland and the LSWR to become the Somerset & Dorset Joint Railway. This event was partly instrumental in bringing about the absorption of the B&ER by the GWR. Perhaps with these changes there might be improvements in the service at Bridgwater that might make a new railway unnecessary?

Four years later matters remained the same as ever. A delegation of Bridgwater businessmen called upon the Somerset & Dorset Joint Committee to explain why a railway should be built to Bridgwater, and endeavoured to get the SDJR to promote it. Within a month, in November 1880, the SDJR decided that they were not prepared to promote the line. This meant that if they wanted the railway badly enough those Bridgwater businessmen would have to look elsewhere for capital. Gone were the days when local landowners and businessmen were willing to subscribe on a grand scale for a local line. Bridgwater would probably only provide a small proportion of the capital. They might canvass existing shareholders of the SDJR, MR and LSWR but they would probably look to the contractor to take a large payment in shares. However, this would not solve the initial problem of raising enough money for the parliamentary deposit and being prepared for another tussle with the B&ER, now GWR.

Either through existing contracts or by the co-operation of R.A. Read and Mr Toogood, a start was made. The Bridgwater party acquired the services of a firm of engineers; Wells, Owen & Elwes. Mr Owen of that company had a useful contact whom he persuaded to join the Bridgwater Railway. This contact was a very shady character, Jasper Wilson Johns, JP and Deputy Lieutenant for Merioneth.

Despite claiming that 'I never promoted a railway in my life', it turned out that he had promoted the Caernarvonshire Railway which was sold to the LNWR at 5 per cent interest in perpetuity. He compared the Bridgwater Railway to the Shrewsbury & Welshpool which was bought by the LNWR and GWR giving 5 per cent guarantee on the stock. Clearly with Johns at the helm the Bridgwater Railway was going to be built to be sold. He was a Director of many small Welsh railways which were of doubtful prosperity. Indeed he was given a roasting before the House of Lords Committee in 1882 about the 'failure' of railway schemes he had been associated with. Be that as it may, Johns served the Bridgwater Railways's needs by finding, with another Director, presumably Mr Browne Martin, the parliamentary deposit. This was rather generous for a shady character, or was it?

One of the most diligent campaigners for the Bridgwater Railway was Alfred Peace. He had been one of the delegation appointed by a town meeting to gain support from the Somerset & Dorset Joint Committee. Even without the SDJC the Bridgwater party were still able to get support from the major landowners such as both West Somerset MPs and Philip Pleydell Bouverie of the banking firm of Ransome Bouverie & Co. and Thomas Broadmead, High Sheriff of Somerset. Unfortunately the MR and LSWR produced a petition against this new Bill but Peace contacted Wyndham Spencer Portal, Deputy Chairman of the LSWR who assured him that they would work the line and that they invariably presented petitions of this sort unless they promoted the Bills themselves. They had everything to gain and nothing to lose. So now the Bridgwater Railway had support in high places and a major company willing to operate the line.

Alfred Peace and Frederick Foster, corn merchant, pursued the traditional Bridgwater case for a new railway, namely the shortage of trucks and the B&ER/GWR grip on the docks. Foster also emphasised that the closure of the Bridgwater B&ER carriage and wagon works had brought great hardship to the artisans.

A strong case for the Bill was put by Edmund Broderip whose father had opposed the line in 1875. Edmund Broderip declared that his own parish of Cossington could send over 100,000 gallons of milk per annum over the new line. His nearest station was Edington, five miles away. He emphasised the difficulty in transporting milk over rough roads in summer which churned the milk about and the contrasting difficulty when for the greater part of the year the road was flooded. He looked forward to an improved communication with London adding that at Edington it was possible to book through to London without paying express fares.

Once again Underdown and Read explained the uselessness of the facility clauses. Underdown stated that common law would give as much protection. He added that it was important to have independence to determine one's own rates instead of having them imposed by the GWR. Read repeated that approaches would have to be made frequently to the Board of Trade and that the S&D could not afford the cost of litigation. As for enlisting LSWR help, Bridgwater traffic was a small thing for them but 'very material to the SDJR who received a minimum rent plus 10 per cent of gross receipts of all traffic in excess of £24 per mile per week'.

The 1882 Bill sought power to raise £135,000 plus borrowing powers for £45,000. The proposed line was virtually the same as the one proposed in 1875. According to Richard Elwes of Wells, Owen & Elwes, engineers to the line, the estimated building cost of £100,000 was generous. When large companies operated these small lines they expected them to be up to their own standards, i.e. able to carry heavy trains at high speeds. Stations, cuttings and embankments needed to be finished in a more expensive manner. If the Bridgwater company was to operate the line itself it could be built for considerably less. He estimated that to maintain a dividend of 4¼ per cent they would have to earn £27 per week per mile. He did not pretend that the agricultural area could produce that but 'Bridgwater is a market, a manufacturing area and an outlet for a large area to the west which has no convenient railway'.

On the possibility of working the line themselves Elwes made it look very simple. He said that three or four engines plus three or four composite carriages were all that was needed, and these could be hired. He added, 'trucks are all over the place, private owners and other railway companies will send trucks over the line. It may cost 60 per cent or 65 per cent of gross receipts as against 50 per cent, but it would give you a better bargaining position when negotiating to sell to a larger company'.

Elwes painted a glowing picture about the prospects of the line and made it all seem simple. R.G. Underdown with his greater experience of railway operation as manager of the Manchester, Sheffield and Lincolnshire made no claim for the profitability of the line as a separate unit. By working the line as part of the S&D it would pay: 'access to Bridgwater cannot be measured by mileage proportion between Edington and Bridgwater. The traffic will go over long distances on the S&D. A division of receipts would pay the S&D itself and the new railway'.

The cold reality of the prospects of the Bridgwater Railway was spelt out by James Grierson, General Manager of the GWR. He explained that on a capital of £120,000 a net revenue of £9,600 would be needed to pay 4 per cent, and that was assuming that working expenses would account for 50 per cent of £9,600, thus leaving £4,800. However 'the SDJR which is a large main line work their system at 78 per cent working expenses. The Bridgwater line working itself could not be worked for less than 90 per cent. It is utterly impossible for the line to pay for itself.' Grierson ably demolished much of the Bridgwater case. He pointed out that Bridgwater's trade was principally an import one and mostly coal at that. The SDJR already had a port for importing coal at Highbridge. The grain and timber traffic at Bridgwater was mostly for places on the GWR system. The passenger traffic at Bridgwater was exceedingly small for a town of 12,000. He believed the facility clauses worked very well and he had received no complaints. Traffic for the SDJR averaged 18 tons a day but even if it was 1,800 tons the GWR had the facilities to handle it.

Grierson's case was backed up by J.C. Wall's parting shot. He considered that Read's demands over the facility clauses were sometimes

. . . outrageous considering the very small amount of traffic . . . We ran a special train in the morning from Highbridge to Bridgwater, the time fixed by the S&D so that traffic handed over to the LSWR in London should arrive at Bridgwater as soon as traffic handed over to the GWR in London. In the evening at about half past four or five an engine and carriage was put on again specially to take the S&D traffic from Bridgwater to Highbridge, the time fixed by the S&D, and a similar service to the one I have explained as Bridgwater and Highbridge was carried between Bridgwater and Yeovil.

He added that neither the MR nor the LSWR or the SDJR had sought this railway. If they thought there was traffic to be got, they would have promoted the line.

Grierson and Wall were very convincing and right in most of what they said. They failed to stop the Bill because they could not disprove before the Committees of Commons and Lords that there was a public demand for the line or that it would not benefit the public. After all, even Mr Underdown agreed that it would 'benefit the public if the line was constructed and sold upon terms which would pay the shareholders a reasonable sum'. This sentiment summed up why the line was really being promoted. No bribes were offered this time to stop the Bill. There was no need to resort to bribery as there was sufficient corruption already among the promoters, more interested in personal gain than public benefit, to cause a further delay of eight years before the line was opened and even more financial embarrassment.

Carter Gilbert Ashill poses with a SDJR delivery van in 1913 at Bridgwater.
Robin Atthill Collection, SDRT Archive

Another carter, this time it is Edmund White. Born in Bridgwater in 1872, Edmund spent most of his life working for the SDJR. *S & DRT Collection, courtesy Mrs P.I. Frost*

Chapter Five
A shotgun wedding

Having obtained their Act of Parliament, the Bridgwater Railway Co. buckled down to appointing officials, raising money, surveying and purchasing land and appointing contractors to build the line. Messrs Wells, Owen & Elwes were officially appointed as Engineers. The bankers were to be Stuckeys who had been of considerable service to the S&D in the past. The Secretary at a salary of £100 was to be W.T. Johns. The solicitor was, of course, W. Toogood who was quick to get his pound of flesh by having an agreement sealed by the Board paying him £800 for parliamentary expenses and £5,000 for the construction of the line. A prospectus was issued to debenture and preference stock holders of the MR, LSWR and SDJR and the inhabitants of the Bridgwater district. Unfortunately the response was disappointing. A year later a new prospectus was then prepared setting out details of agreements made with the LSWR and MR. The public response to the second prospectus was virtually nil.

By May 1884 about £40,000 share capital had been subscribed, but considerably more was needed before contractors could be safely instructed to commence work. Another problem was that an agreement for a contract to build the line for cash had been made with Eckersley & Bayliss. Clearly if the line was to be built within the time limit stipulated by Act of Parliament this agreement had to be renegotiated, because the Bridgwater company was not going to be able to raise sufficient capital from the public.

Eckersley & Bayliss must have been reluctant to lose the opportunity of a cash contract. The cost of relieving them of the contract was £6,500 in fully paid up shares and £500 cash. Read then set about finding a contractor who would construct the line, purchase the land, deposit £20,000 with the operating company for additional works, pay 4½ per cent interest on the capital already subscribed until six months after the opening of the line, all in return for £96,190 of the unissued shares, £45,000 in 4 per cent debenture stock and £5,000 in cash. Read found a contractor, G.C. Harvey, willing to meet these terms and the proposed deal was submitted to the Board for consideration. The Board was willing to accept G.C. Harvey's offer, but stipulated a number of provisos. The details of what followed are unknown but the proposed deal collapsed. Read also resigned, but whether it was owing to the collapse of this deal or his general dissatisfaction with the Board or for other reasons it is difficult to say.

Several would-be contractors approached the company but no deal materialised. One, Mr Rankin, even offered to find a suitable contractor providing he was paid a commission of £1,500! Meanwhile time was slipping by, the share capital had not significantly increased and interest was owing to those who had already subscribed. The shareholders, mostly SDJR stockholders, became restless and complained. The Board then sent a letter, in December 1885, to the shareholders and explained that a Bill was being prepared seeking an extension of the time limit and power to issue preference stock.

The letter did not quell the unrest. In April 1886 a special meeting was called at which the shareholders expressed their dissatisfaction and asked the Board to resign with the exception of Mr Peace 'in whom they had the utmost confidence'. They then elected to the Board H.H.P. Bouverie as Chairman and, once again, R.A. Read.

It fell chiefly to Read to have to explain before the Parliamentary committees the reasons why the Bridgwater Railway Co. wanted extra time in which to complete the line. One of the reasons was financial mismanagement, although Read pointed out to the committees that he was not involved. The Parliamentary Committee were especially critical of the fact that £30,000 had been spent with nothing to show for it. Amongst this was a figure of £12,000 for preliminary and parliamentary expenses for a Bill that was before Parliament for just two days. The most scandalous part of this had been £6,000 in shares paid to those gentlemen, J.W. Johns and another, who had made the Parliamentary deposit of £6,000 in Consuls which, when released, would return to Johns and his accomplice. Thus for risking their own funds for the Parliamentary deposit they had earned 100 per cent i.e. the £6,000 in shares plus of course the legitimate interest that Consuls earned. Although he did not spell it out, perhaps the £5,800 paid to Toogood comprised the rest of the 'preliminary and parliamentary expenses'. Then there was £7,000 paid to discharge Eckersley & Bayliss. The prospectus cost £3,000–£4,000. Roughly the same sum had been paid to shareholders as interest. Engineering costs had been £2,500. Finally there was £11,000 –£12,000 in the bank.

Owen, the Engineer, repeated what he had said in 1882 about being able to build the line for considerably less than the estimate of £120,000, which was largely determined by LSWR's requirements. To illustrate his point he mentioned that they were unable to use timber for bridges or stations, and as Bridgwater would be a terminal station for the whole S&D system this station would cost £12,000–£14,000 and perhaps more.

By the time the 1886 Extension Bill reached the House of Lords, Read was able to inform their lordships that the LSWR had reduced their requirements and that a 'contractor of very high standing' had been found to build the railway for £74,000, and that as the land would not cost more than £17,000 a large saving would be made. Read's astuteness had gained time and saved the Bridgwater Railway. Francis Fox of the B&ER would have been justified in saying 'I told you so!'

However, no contract had been signed and sealed at this stage although one was urgently required to save future embarrassment. What happened was that a Mr Young approached the company and said that he could secure the completion of the line for the unissued £60,000 of the 4 per cent preference shares, the balance of the unissued £29,390 ordinary stock and the £45,000 debenture stock, providing the Directors could obtain a transfer from the present shareholders of one third of their holding to the persons who found the new capital. The price was high, but they had to get this line built, so by July 1887 the Board had agreed to conclude a contract along those lines with a contractor indicated by Mr Young. A few months later Mr Young asked the company to present another Bill to Parliament changing the 4 per cent preference stock to 4½ per cent. This was duly done. Also 62 shareholders were persuaded to part with a third of their shares.

On 1st March, 1888 a contract was sealed with John Morris, W. Woolley and A. Young for the construction of the line. The contractors were now the virtual owners. The Board, who since 1885 had controlled the destinies of the Bridgwater Railway in the public interest (even if that meant the Bridgwater merchants and the SDJR, determined to get their line) had sold out to a group whose sole motive was monetary gain. The difference between the figures quoted by Read to Parliament of £74,000 plus £17,000 and the share payment to the contractors less liabilities of about £11,000 indicate a profit, albeit a paper one, of between £40,000 and £50,000. The Board was a reluctant bride in a shotgun marriage. It is little wonder that the company's minutes refer to this contract as the 'Contract with the Capitalists'. Six months later in October 1888 the deal still seems to have rankled with the Secretary when he recorded the Directors' approval of the Commissioners of Sewers stipulations for the bridge to cross the South Drain 'subject to the consent of the capitalists'.

Mr. BUXTON and FAMILY.

(Contractor for the Bridgwater Railway)

'Mr. Buxton and Family, Contractor for the Bridgwater Railway.' As his name does not appear in surviving Bridgwater Railway archives, the conclusion must be that this sporting gentleman had a contract with the 'capitalists' to build the line.   *S & DRT Collection*

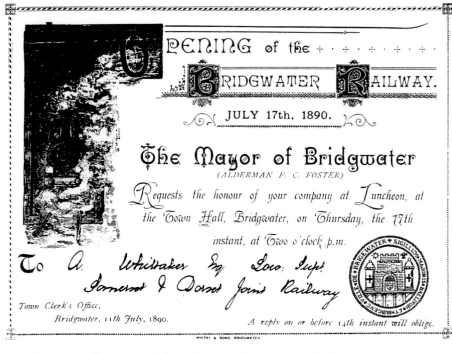

OPENING of the

BRIDGWATER RAILWAY.

JULY 17th, 1890.

The Mayor of Bridgwater
(ALDERMAN F. C. FOSTER)

Requests the honour of your company at Luncheon, at the Town Hall, Bridgwater, on Thursday, the 17th instant, at Two o'clock p.m.

To A. Whittaker Esq Loco. Supt Somerset & Dorset Joint Railway

Town Clerk's Office,
Bridgwater, 11th July, 1890.

A reply on or before 14th instant will oblige.

Invitation to the opening of the Bridgwater Railway sent to Alfred Whittaker, Locomotive Superintendent of the Somerset & Dorset Joint Railway.

Whittaker Collection, courtesy of Peter McGhie

Menu card for the Luncheon to mark the opening of the Bridgwater Railway.

Whittaker Collection, courtesy of Peter McGhie

OPENING OF THE

Bridgwater Railway.

LUNCHEON

At the TOWN HALL, BRIDGWATER,

By invitation of the Worshipful the Mayor of Bridgwater (ALDERMAN F. C. FOSTER).

MENU.

Turkey a la Royall.   Roast Lamb.
Veal and Ham Pies.   Pigeon Pies.   Roast Beef.
Braized Beef.   Gelantine of Veal.   Hams.
Roast Chicken.   Tongues.   Roast Ducks.
Salads—Mayonaise.

Cherry Tart.   Plum Tart.
Raspberry and Currant Tart.   Fruit Jellies.
Maraschino Jelly.   Vanella Cream.
Charlotte Russe.   Strawberries and Cream.

Cheese and Butter.

Chapter Six
Success at last

In a little over two years from the signing of the contract the line was opened. During this time the SDJR stepped in to replace the LSWR as the operating company for an experimental three-year period. The same company agreed to carry out interlocking alterations at Edington Junction that had been recommended by Col Rich, the Board of Trade Inspector, so that, 'local trains, that start and arrive at the Dock platform line which is at the back of the S&DR Co.'s Edington down platform, need not cross onto the S&D Rly.' He also stated that the distant signals should be placed so as to be seen from the line. Three days before this, Henry Bouverie and E.B. Read, Chairman and Secretary respectively, signed an undertaking that the railway would be operated by Tyer's Electric Staff Tablet System and that all engines except those running funnel first would stop at Cossington station.

The opening day dawned ten days after Rich's report, on 21st July, 1890. By 9.00 am it had started to rain, and this continued all day. A procession that had been planned in Bridgwater was cancelled so the Mayor and Corporation were driven to the station, where a large crowd had gathered to welcome the first train. The V.I.P.'s who disembarked were dined at the Town Hall in grand style. The streets of Bridgwater were decorated with flags. An evergreen arch had been erected at the end of Monmouth Street with banners proclaiming 'prosperity to the Town and Trade of Bridgwater', and 'Success to the New Railway'.

All was not to be gloomy. Between the opening and the purchasing of the line by the LSWR in 1921, the preference shareholders regularly received their 4½ per cent dividend and during the first decade of the 20th century the ordinary stock reached the heady heights of 5½ per cent in 1902, 6 per cent in 1904 and £6.6.0 per cent in 1908. When one bears in mind the few people who owned stock and the fact that their dividends were guaranteed under the terms of the lease arranged with the LSWR and taken up by the SDJR, the 'profits' do not reflect the health of the Bridgwater Railway as such, but rather the prosperity of the SDJR system backed up by the MR and the LSWR.

The first 10 years of the Bridgwater Railway were very active times. Various teething problems had to be sorted out and facilities added. Under the terms of the agreement with the SDJR, £5,000 had to be deposited with the operating company to cover the provision of unforeseen facilities. Items such as a 10-ton crane; cattle pens; a stable, scullery and W.C. at the Bridgwater stationmaster's house; additional bedrooms in the four crossing cottages; were all charged to the deposit in 1891. The opportunity was taken to purchase materials surplus to the contractor's requirements: sleepers, chairs, 82 lb rails, fish bolts, spikes, platelayers huts, tool chests and a hut worth £111 11s. 6d. The Engineer's working plans and sections together with tracings of the bridges, stations and other structures were also offered to the company. A parcels and goods receiving office was rented in Bridgwater, while an agreement with Mr Peace was arranged whereby he would provide a collection and delivery service for goods and parcels at Bridgwater. Despite the fact that SDJR were operating the railway their coaching stock was somewhat stretched in 1891, so a temporary loan of carriages was sought from the LSWR.

The SDJR reconsidered the lease in 1893. The three-year experimental period was over and they did not feel confident enough to renew over a long period of time so they decided on a 12 months extension after which they would reconsider the position. Meanwhile additional sidings and cattle pens were installed at Cossington. At the same time Messrs Board's leased 60 acres for 42 years at Cossington to develop a limestone quarry. They also planned to build a lime and cement works at Bridgwater. The SDJR agreed to connect sidings for Board's at both places provided Board's paid 9d. a ton for owner's wagons between Bridgwater and Cossington. This was of course a boon to the railway. It had attracted new business which would benefit the railway as well as Cossington and Bridgwater.

Another firm that might have brought some traffic to the railway was the Bear Creek Oil Co. They sought permission to build a warehouse for the storage and distribution of petrol on land adjoining the steam crane wharf. The dock weighing-machine was situated at the far end of the dock line some 1½ miles from the station. As this was inconvenient, the weighbridge was moved to the station yard. Increased revenue was earned at Bridgwater station by renting the right to erect advertisement boards to Smith & Sons who were charged 5 per cent of their bookstall and 50 per cent of their advertising receipts. One consequence of this was that poor Mr Peace who had been advertising free of charge on the stations now had to remove his adverts. There were few perks in a Bridgwater Railway directorship.

Mr Peace's bad luck continued into 1894 when the SDJR terminated his carting agency and determined to do their own carting in Bridgwater. A timber drug and spring dray were bought from Mr Peace for £40. Two horses were needed, and by slight alteration to the existing stable occupied by the shunting horse the extra stock could be accomodated. Meanwhile Messrs Board's decided that the siding into their proposed quarry would be more convenient if it faced the opposite direction to the way agreed the previous year. The SDJR agreed to lay the siding in accordance with Board's wishes at a cost of £470 spread over 10 years, although Board's did get their wagon tonnage rate reduced by a penny. Another new industry was attracted in 1894 when a Liverpudlian soap manufacturer, Mr Stark, wished to rent a piece of waste land adjoining the wharf at Bridgwater for a slime bed. Things were now looking a bit brighter for the line so the SDJR decided to renew their lease for a further three years.

Further siding changes were made at Cossington in 1896. It was realised that cattle traffic was being diverted away from Cossington because the existing siding connection necessitated wagons en route to Edington going to Bridgwater first.

When the lease came up for review in 1897 it was renewed only for one year after which, to lighten the burden of the line, the SDJR managed to persuade the LSWR to bear a third of the difference between the cost of working and the amount allowed under the agreement between the LSWR and the Bridgwater Railway for working the line, namely 50 per cent of the receipts. The SDJR would bear the other two-thirds of the loss!

Working losses there may have been but traffic was increasing sufficiently to necessitate alterations to the working arrangements that required an extra engine to be stabled at Bridgwater in 1898. As the existing engine shed only had room for one engine, the shed was extended and an additional coal siding was installed. An extra siding and a 5-ton crane were installed at Bridgwater the following year, and in 1900 the Bear Creek Oil Co. expanded their interests by building two oil tanks there.

It was decided in 1899 by the officers of the Somerset & Dorset Joint Committee that two extra sidings were needed at Edington to cope with Bridgwater traffic. These extra sidings are a bit of a puzzle because the later maps of the arrangements at Edington do not appear to be significantly different from the jigsaw remnants of the plan accompanying the Board of Trade report in 1890. At first sight it would appear that these two sidings were built, because in November 1899 the Directors approved the construction of the sidings at an estimated cost of £224, and by April 1901 the Bridgwater Railway's deposit account was charged £151 for 'siding accomodation at Edington'. A charge that was 33 per cent cheaper than the estimate does indicate some rationalisation. A possible explanation is that instead of actually building two extra sidings, the existing siding accommodation at Edington was extended.

Since 1909, 255 ft of the wharf at Bridgwater had ceased to be used and had been fenced off. It had become so dilapidated by 1912 that it was decided, after discussions between the Bridgwater Railway, the SDJR and the Bridgwater Navigation Trustees, to remove the wharf and replace it with mooring posts on the understanding that if future traffic required it, a wharf would be re-instated.

Thereafter official records of activity on the Bridgwater Railway virtually cease until after the Great War. There is one entry only for the war years, recording permission for the War Office to store hay alongside the wharf branch at Bridgwater. During the war the nation's railways had been controlled by the Railway Executive Committee. The overall success of the REC in unifying the railway network and removing many of the disadvantages of the 'competitive' system in a wartime economy convinced many people that the railways should be run as one system.

This was too revolutionary a move for the early post-war years, especially with the memories of the Bolshevik revolution fresh in establishment minds. The typical English compromise emerged therefore with the grouping of the railways into four major companies. While the MR and LSWR were merged into the LMS and SR respectively, the line that they leased jointly maintained a separate identity. The Bridgwater Railway however, lost its identity before the Grouping. Under the Railways Act of 1921 it was absorbed by the LSWR. The existing working arrangements were cancelled and the Bridgwater Railway was considered as part of the SDJR. The MR was to pay the LSWR £8,000 per annum for the advantages of the Bridgwater traffic coming their way.

The Bridgwater Railway had existed for a little over 30 years. It had been an 'independent' line in name only, having been promoted as an extension to the SDJR system, built as a contractor's line, leased to the SDJR, and eventually absorbed by the LSWR. From 1922 until its closure in 1952 it was an increasing financial drain for, in turn, the SDJR, the SR and the LMS and BR.

Edmund White is the carter in this early view of Bridgwater station. Next door to the station building is the station master's house and behind the delivery van is the roof of No.17 Bristol Road, Edmund's daughter's house, where he died aged 56 in 1930.

S & DRT Collection, courtesy Mrs. P.I. Frost

Edmund White appears again on the extreme left of the back row in this group photo on the concourse at Bridgwater station. Station master Hawkins is seated in the centre of the middle row. The tarpaulin on the van in the background advertises Peace's furniture removals, suggesting that this photo may date from the time when Alfred Peace was carting agent for the SDJR in Bridgwater, i.e. 1890–4.

S & DRT Collection, courtesy Mrs. P.I. Frost

Chapter Seven

The Bridgwater, Stowey & Stogursey Light Railway

Had the Bridgwater Railway been mooted in the closing years of the 19th century, it might have been constructed as a light railway. Such railways were built to less exacting standards, using lighter section rails, fewer facilities and with traffic being restricted in weight and speed. Despite the application of light railways, especially in agrarian areas, having been advocated as early as the 1840s in this country, the pioneering work was carried out in France and Belgium where local governments were allowed to finance construction out of taxation. Not until the Local Government Act of 1888 were county rates able to be levied in this country for rural services. Board of Trade encouragement followed and in 1896 the Light Railway Act received its Royal Assent.

Unfortunately, very little use was made of the Act by the County Councils, mainly because the schemes were too expensive, tending to be in excess of £7,000 per mile in contrast to less than £3,000 per mile in the Low Countries. Thus it was left to enthusiastic individuals or groups to promote light railways, and if they could not persuade County Councils to back them then perhaps they could find a more sympathetic champion in the established railway companies. The Somerset & Dorset Railway was approached by several Light Railway promoters but declined to back any of them. One of these schemes, The Bridgwater, Stowey & Stogursey Light Railway, was planned to connect with the Bridgwater Railway. An examination of this scheme illustrates the light railway concept and some of the naivety that made them financially unviable.

The Directors of the Bridgwater, Stowey & Stogursey Light Railway, who obtained their Order from the Light Railway Commissioners in 1901, were Henry Bouverie, John Morris, Alfred Peace, Robert A. Read and Alexander Young. It is perhaps surprising that this group of gentlemen, especially with R.A. Read among their number, did not succeed in building the proposed line. Starting from Stogursey, it was to have been built in a southerly direction on the east side of the main road from Stogursey to Nether Stowey, thence in an easterly direction to the north-west of Fiddington, to the south of Bolam Bridge, to the north-east of Cannington and to the south of Chilton Trinity. It would have terminated in a junction with the Bridgwater Railway, 350 yards from the latter's terminus.

Commonplace light railway restrictions were included in the Order, restricting axle-weights to 12 tons, or 14 tons if the rail weight was not less than 60 lb. per yard. Speeds were to be no more than 25 mph or 20 mph when passing a gradient steeper than 1 in 50, or 10 mph on curves less than 9 chains. Turntables were not deemed necessary but engines running tender first were to be restricted to no more than 15 mph. There were to be signals at crossing points, plus distant signals if the home signals could not be seen from a distance of ¼-mile. Signals had to be fail-safe and interlocked with the relevant points. Platforms were to be built unless carriages were fitted with 'proper and convenient means of access' to ground level. The railway company did not have to provide shelters or conveniences. All these stipula-

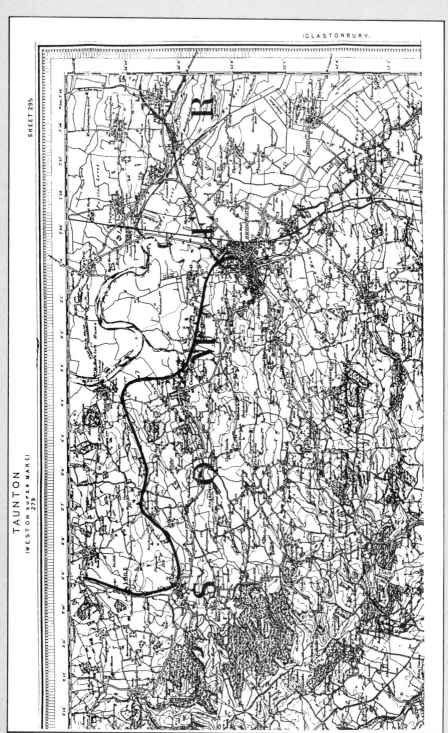

Proposed route of the Bridgwater, Stowey & Stogursey Light Railway superimposed on a 1" O.S. map.
Reproduced by courtesy of the Public Record Office, Kew

tions were conducive to keeping costs at a minimum for a railway serving a sparsely populated area, on which the traffic would be light, and yet at the same time they had due regard for the safe operating of the line.

The aspect of the railway which ensured that it would be too expensive for it to materialise as a light railway was the need to cross the River Parrett if it was to join the Bridgwater Railway. It was planned to do this by tunnelling to a depth of 4 ft 6 in. under the river bed to meet the minimum requirements of Bridgwater Corporation for dredging purposes. To reach that modest depth, the line would descend from the west on gradients of 1 in 88 and 1 in 30 while the gradients on the east would be 1 in 55 and 1 in 30. In the middle of the tunnel there was to be a 30 yards-length on the level.

When the plan for the tunnel was submitted to Col Yorke of the Board of Trade, he considered that the steep inclines combined with the 30 yards on the level would be difficult to work and would lead to couplings snapping. Furthermore, the liability of the adjacent land to flooding would cause costly drainage problems. Consequently the plans were modified and re-submitted but this time Col Yorke's objective observations gave way to scathing criticisms. Although the depth of the tunnel had been lowered to 9 ft below the river bed, and brick inverts and massive concrete walls planned to combat the danger from flooding, and the 30 yards of level track replaced by a vertical curve, 'the 1 in 30 gradients remain. The Mersey Railway has similar gradients. The Mersey Railway has in consequence been a financial failure.' It was now also proposed to build sidings at each end of the tunnel so that trains could be divided to reduce the load that an engine would have to haul through the tunnel.

'This means delay and expense', fumed Yorke, 'and will necessitate signals and signalmen at each end . . . and no mixed train should be allowed to enter the tunnel.' As the diameter of the tunnel was only 16 ft Yorke calculated that the rails would have to be lowered to accommodate a 'full-sized railway carriage', until the lower rail flange would only be six inches above the iron-lining of the tunnel. 'I do not see how it will be possible to construct a satisfactory permanent way', Yorke went on, 'the rails will soon be hammered to pieces.' His criticism culminated in a damning indictment, 'a tunnel of this description . . . will cost at least £40,000, and . . . will form an impediment to the economical working of the traffic (and) is quite unsuited to a light railway.' The Bridgwater, Stowey & Stogursey Light Railway estimated its total costs to be £85,704 12s. 6d. which worked out at approximately £7,728 per mile which although comparable with other British light railways was still much more expensive than its continental counterparts.

Despite these criticisms the Board of Trade did not deny the company its Order, but as this light railway was not constructed, one must conclude that the promoters were unable to attract sufficient investment to make it worthwhile to proceed with the project. As the tunnel costs accounted for nearly half of the total estimated costs, it is necessary to consider if there was a realistic alternative.

In 1899 residents of West Somerset had presented a memorandum to the Somerset & Dorset Joint Committee requesting that the Somerset & Dorset line be extended from Bridgwater to Watchet and Exeter. The Joint Commit-

Engineer's drawings showing arrangements for the proposed tunnel under the River Parrett. The inclines in this tunnel were to have been 1 in 30.

Reproduced by courtesy of the Public Record Office, Kew

tee declined to act on the memorandum and it is not difficult to speculate why. Exeter was already served by both the LSWR and the GWR and a route from Bridgwater to Exeter would duplicate the existing GWR line. Even if the capital could be raised, it is difficult to envisualise the SDJR stimulating significantly extra traffic and at best would have had 50 per cent of the business currently carried by the well-established GWR. Watchet had been served by the West Somerset line since the 1860s, giving that part of Somerset communication with the county town, Taunton. So the Somerset & Dorset did not want the expense of entering 'new' territory that was already served by the GWR. Also, it was a rural area whose traffic was unlikely to produce reasonable returns on capital invested. Nevertheless, there was a perceived need for rail communication with Bridgwater by people who lived between Watchet and that market town. Perhaps by considering some of the personalities involved we may understand the motives behind the line.

Poor people do not live in Pall Mall. Henry Hales Pleydell Bouverie was a member of a prominent banking family and his address was No.1 Pall Mall. He was also Chairman of the Bridgwater Railway and the leading promoter of the Bridgwater, Stowey & Stogursey Light Railway which would pass almost within a mile of his country seat, Brymore. His family also had old connections with the Somerset & Dorset Railway, Philip Bouverie having been the first Chairman of the Somerset Central Railway.

Promoters two and three were John Morris and Alexander Young, two of the contractors who built the Bridgwater Railway and, consequently, major shareholders of that undertaking. Promoter number four was Alfred Peace who had campaigned vigorously for the Bridgwater Railway and was also a Director. Number five was Robert Arthur Read, the erstwhile General Manager of the Somerset & Dorset whose dynamism was largely responsible for the manifestation of the Bridgwater Railway. Thus all the major promoters were Bridgwater Railway men. No matter how philanthropic they may have been in attempting to provide the Stowey, Stogursey and Cannington districts with railway communication, their competitive instincts would ensure that it should have a junction with the Bridgwater Railway.

Had the Light Railway almost halved its costs by terminating on the west side of the River Parrett, it would have remained a self-contained railway with no physical connection with another. The rural communities it would serve would still be provided with access to their nearest market town, while passengers who wished to travel by rail further afield would have the inconvenience of a walk to either the Bridgwater Railway station or the GWR line. Such a dislocation for goods traffic however would have been ludicrous. An alternative might have been to seek an agreement to have running powers over the telescopic bridge, which would have given the Light Railway access to the Great Western station. This may well have involved considerable expense in driving the Light Railway through an urban area, resulting in higher land-costs and compensation and would have subjected the Light Railway timetable to disruption by tides, as these determined the opening times of the telescopic bridge. Even if the GWR was willing to accommodate the possibility, it was not an ideal answer to the Light Railway's need for a junction and, besides, for the Bridgwater Railway men a union with the opposition was probably out of the question.

Why not build a bridge across the River Parrett? To avoid the cost of approaching the bridge through an urban area and having a junction with the Bridgwater Railway meant crossing the Parrett at about the same place as the proposed tunnel. That location was down river from the dock entrance. The Port and Navigation Committee of Bridgwater Corporation would not have tolerated an obstruction to shipping *en route* to or from their docks. A bridge high enough to clear the masts of ships at spring tides would have involved costly earthworks on either side of the Parrett, quite beyond the scope of a light railway. A telescopic bridge or a bascule bridge, while avoiding the expensive approaches, would have been potential navigation hazards because there was always the possibility that they could fail to open. That may seem a negative stance, but it would have been sufficient reason for parties opposed to the idea to cause a storm sufficient to turn opinion against the Light Railway, and subsequently effect investment.

The Bridgwater, Stowey & Stogursey Light Railway simply was not built because its promoters were Bridgwater Railway men who clearly needed to get that line across the Parrett. A bridge was out of the question, and the design of the tunnel so defective and costly that Col Yorke was unequivical in his condemnation. Without the support of the Somerset & Dorset Joint Committee, this line could not be financed or built. When the promoters approached the SDJC in 1903 with the suggestion that the latter construct and work the light railway, the Committee agreed that the idea 'be not entertained'. That is as far as the Bridgwater, Stowey & Stogursey Light Railway reached; a courageous concept that fostered a paper exercise and no more, for not a sod was turned.

Vulcan 0–4–4T No.55 fitted for push-pull working, as rebuilt in 1925 with a G5½ boiler with Belpaire firebox, straight sided Deeley chimney with capuchon and widened cab. Note Whittaker's apparatus attached to the bunker for exchanging the single-line tablet.
L&GRP Collection, courtesy David & Charles Ltd

Chapter Eight
Decline and fall

The first 14 years of the 20th century formed the golden era of Britain's railways. Never again were the railways to carry the amount of freight that they had carried in 1913. After the brief post war boom a trade depression set in during 1921 accompanied by a major coal strike. Competition from road transport was rapidly making itself felt. Operating costs had also risen dramatically and a significant part of this was increased labour costs. Thus all the major railway companies were looking for economies and the Bridgwater Railway did not escape.

In 1922 an inquiry into the costs of working and maintaining the SDJR had this to say of the Bridgwater line:

Bridgwater Loco: Three drivers, three firemen and one cleaner are stationed at this depot and a shunting engine is employed daily. Recommend branch should be closed at night and the necessary work performed by the branch engine and all other power cancelled, as only 25 wagons per day are dealt with, saving one set of men.

Edington Junction: Expenses up 187 per cent. Assistance to cover the hours of the booking clerk at this station is provided from Bridgwater. Recommend that this be withdrawn, and the early and late porters to book any passengers who use the early and late trains. This will enable a clerk to be saved at Bridgwater; one porter can be withdrawn. Saving per annum £138.

Bridgwater: Expenses up 161 per cent. The traffic at this station has decreased to a very considerable extent without the staff being much reduced. Recommend: the clerk who now performs his duty at Edington Junction to be relieved of this duty, which in addition to the loss of traffic will admit of two clerks being saved at Bridgwater. One guard to be withdrawn and two porters to be trained as porter-guards to take the early and late train service. The working foreman to be withdrawn. One of the goods porters to be graded as checker. One carman, one horse and van to be dispensed with. Savings £1008.

Cossington: Expenses up 423 per cent. Recommend one porter to be withdrawn. Savings £138.

The gloom indicated by this report was not to be found everywhere. In 1923 the residents of the village of Bawdrip successfully petitioned for a halt. The 140 ft reinforced concrete platform attracted so much passenger traffic (2,185 passengers between 7th July and 29th September) that a platform shelter was also provided the following year.

By the time of the Railway Grouping £1,679 11s. 9d. was all that remained of the £5,000 that the Bridgwater Railway had deposited with the SDJR for capital expenditure. It was now agreed that when that sum was exhausted the SR would provide the necessary works and charge the SDJR 5 per cent interest per year. The economies in motive power meant that the engine shed was now disused. In 1928 it began to earn its keep again by being let to the local Co-op for £20 per annum. The siding leading to the shed was shortened by 1 chain 50 links.

The SDJR could no longer ignore the internal combustion engine and its advantages. In 1929 a 2-ton 'Karrier' was bought for £510 to replace two carmen, three horses and four horse-drawn vehicles. It was hoped that this would increase the efficiency of collection and delivery services, but to avoid putting all their eggs in one basket the SDJR retained one horse team.

The Bridgwater line came close to closure in 1933. Owing to a heavy fall in receipts on the whole SDJR system between 1931 and 1933 occasioned by road competition, the general trade depression, national economy in road making and the loss of the valuable SR rail traffic from South Wales through Highbridge, serious consideration was given to closing the Wells and Bridgwater lines. It was decided not to close these lines but to think of ways of improving the net revenue by perhaps increasing the frequency of the passenger services, stopping for passengers at level crossings and other convenient points and using light rail car units to allow passengers to get on or off at suitably levelled places.

Another blow to the line in 1933 was Messrs Board's notice to end the siding agreement at Cossington, although this was not completely removed until 1940. The same year, 1933, also saw the removal of the crossover road at Cossington as its dilapidated condition was a potential cause of derailment.

The formation of the Milk Marketing Board also caused a fall in the SDJR milk traffic. As a consequence of this the current operating methods were reviewed. Further economies were sought by investigating the possibilities of pooling carting arrangements with the GWR at Bridgwater. This possibility was eventually rejected because it was thought to be too difficult to organise and supervise. Meanwhile Bridgwater station was renovated with improvements to the Goods Office and the demolition of the coal stage and stable. Edington was renovated three years later in 1937.

The possibility of closing the Bridgwater branch came up again in 1940 but the matter was postponed because of the war. Certainly the war brought a period of renewed activity as freight traffic increased by over 22 per cent during the last quarter of 1939.

In 1942 the disused lines leading to the wharf at Bridgwater and the siding to Barham's works were recovered. The 24 ft by 10 ft goods office was considered too small by 1946 and a decision was taken to extend it. But this was a last gasp of capital infusion into the Bridgwater line. After the war further consideration to close the line was postponed until after nationalisation. Dwindling traffic receipts led to the closure of the line for passenger traffic in December 1952. Freight was carried over the line until October 1954 when the Bridgwater branch was closed completely. Bridgwater station was linked with the Western Region dock branch and was used as a goods station until 7th July, 1962.

A very early view of Edington Junction as evidenced by the clean paintwork and the ladies' fashions. The carriages in the bay platform are lit by oil and the leading vehicle has a birdcage roof reminiscent of a J. Wright 3rd brake of 1862. It may be that these carriages were those that the SDJR borrowed from LSWR in 1891 to operate the Bridgwater Railway. Although indistinct, the locomotive seems to have external framing which would suggest that this is one of the two re-built George England engines, 17A or 18A, both of which were withdrawn in 1897. This photograph is an example of how elderly rolling stock was relegated to short branch line traffic.

S&DRT Collection

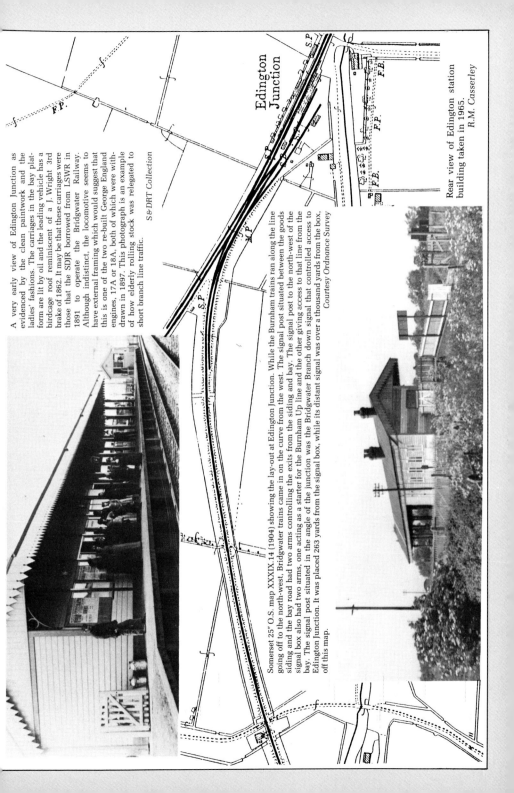

Edington Junction

Somerset 25" O.S. map XXXIX.14 (1904) showing the lay-out at Edington Junction. While the Burnham trains ran along the line going off to the north-west, Bridgwater trains came in on the curve from the west. The signal post situated between the goods siding and the bay road had two arms controlling the exits from the siding and bay. The signal post to the north-west of the signal box also had two arms, one acting as a starter for the Burnham Up line and the other giving access to that line from the bay. The signal post situated in the angle of the junction was the Bridgwater Branch down signal that controlled access to Edington Junction. It was placed 263 yards from the signal box, while its distant signal was over a thousand yards from the box, off this map.

Courtesy Ordnance Survey

Rear view of Edington station building taken in 1965.

R.M. Casserley

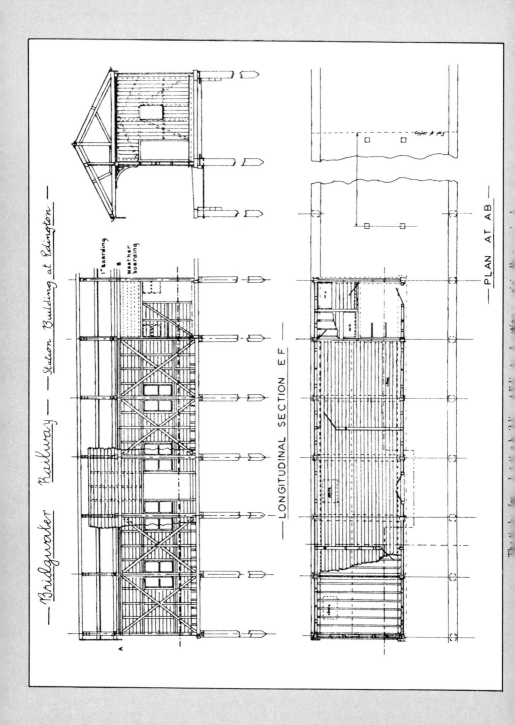

Bridgwater Railway — Station Building at Edington —

1" boarding
&
weather boarding

— LONGITUDINAL SECTION E F —

— PLAN AT AB —

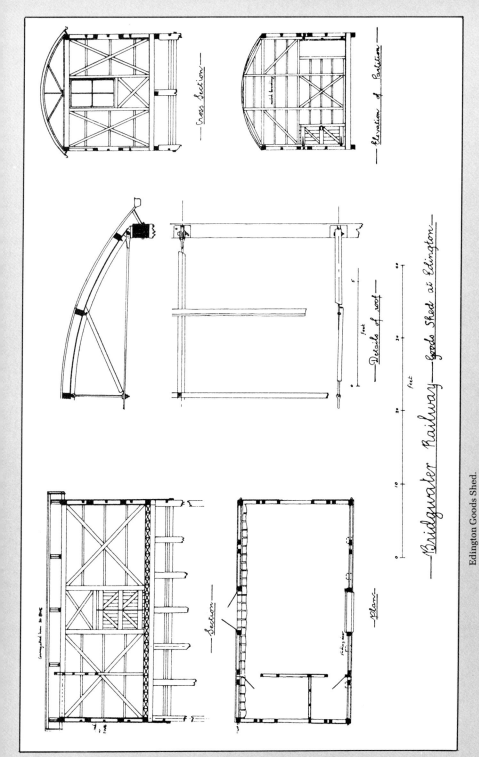

— Cross Section —

— Elevation of Partition —

— Details of roof —

— Bridgwater Railway — Goods Shed at Edington —

— Section —

— Plan —

Edington Goods Shed.

Drawing by Neil Pankhurst based on Contractors' drawing, courtesy of British Rail

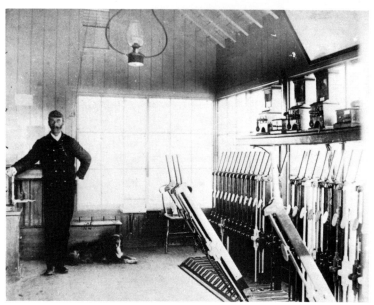

This view of the interior of Edington Junction signal box was possibly taken by William Buck when the box was newly opened. Buck was the chief draughtsman of Dutton & Co. and the designer of the lever-frame incorporated in this box. He included this photograph in his unpublished memoirs.

The signalman's right hand rests on the Tyer's No.6 tablet instrument. On the shelf are Tyer's block instruments which, with the staff & ticket system, controlled the main line. The non-pegging instruments were fitted with handles that enabled them to be used as single needle telegraphs to transmit messages.   *(S. Johnson, SRS Newsletter No.101) S & DRT Collection*

This exterior view of Edington Junction signal box was probably taken on the same occasion as the previous photograph. It would be interesting to know who the gentlemen were.

S & DRT Collection

EDINGTON ROAD JUNCTION

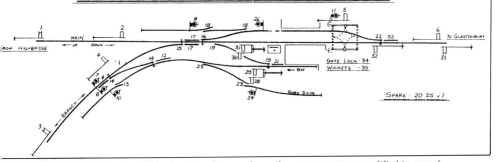

Edington Road Junction. This signalling diagram shows the arrangements as modified in accordance with the requirements of the Board of Trade inspector prior to the opening of the line in 1890. The access to the bay line was upgraded by putting in facing point lock 12, traps 13 and 23, disc signal 24. Meanwhile, facing point lock 20 protecting point 19, and disc signals 25 and 27 protecting points 16 & 19, were removed. *Drawing by Stuart Johnson*

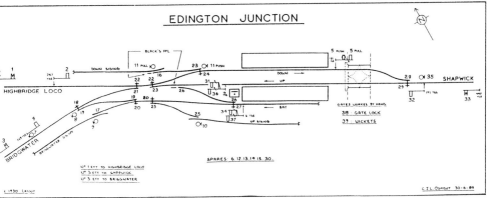

At a later date the Dutton frame was replaced by a conventional LSWR Stevens frame. This diagram shows the arrangements as in 1930. *Drawing by Chris Osment*

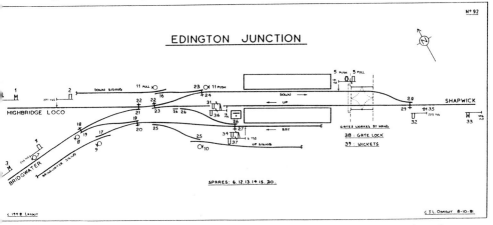

This signalling diagram dated 1948 indicates that signals 1, 2, 4, 32 and 33 had been relocated since 1930. *Drawing by Chris Osment*

The timber-framed station building and canopy at Edington Junction on the island platform.
SDRT Archive

Edington Junction with down platform on the right and the island platform on the left. Beyond the signal box a Bridgwater train is being shunted. As the bay road is occupied by goods wagons, the passenger train will have to use the up main line platform.
L&GRP Collection, courtesy David & Charles

Chapter Nine
Description of the line

The Bridgwater Railway began its route to Bridgwater at Edington Road on the old Somerset Central section of the Somerset & Dorset Joint Railway. The SDJR Evercreech-Burnham line and its run-round loop served the main platforms, the Bridgwater Railway line occupying the bay platform. It seems likely however, that trains arriving from Bridgwater stopped at the down main platform, engines would then run round and pull the train back onto the Bridgwater line before reversing into the bay from which Bridgwater trains would depart. A siding ran parallel to the Bridgwater branch and could serve as a headshunt to both the bay platform and the goods siding.

Recently, engineer's drawings for many of the buildings constructed on the Bridgwater Railway have come to light, along with what appears to be some drawings for proposed structures that were not in fact built. One of the latter was for a platform shelter at Edington with a bench seat situated around three sides of an enclosed shelter occupying two bays of a gabled roof awning. That drawing does give the impression that it was an alternative suggestion to the one that was adopted on the island platform, in that a similar awning was constructed, but instead of including a seated shelter there was a weather-boarded timber-framed station building that included a booking office, a general waiting room, a ladies waiting room and conveniences. The awning was designed to have a corrugated iron covering, and the whole structure covered the whole width of the 20 ft platform which was based on 10 in. × 10 in. piles set at 9 ft intervals, 8 ft under the station building, revetted internally with old sleepers capped with 12 in. × 6 in. timber, dry filled and topped with gravel.

Adjacent to the goods siding was a 33 ft 10 in. by 16 ft 6 in. goods shed, once again timber-framed, but covered in corrugated iron and sporting an arc roof supported by 4 in. × 4 in. purlins resting on T-iron rafters with iron rod tie-bar and king-post and braced with angle-iron. A matchboarding partition 6 ft 6 in. in from one end allowed for a small office and a cupboard. A sliding door with a 5 ft aperture faced the siding while double outward-opening doors enabled goods to be off-loaded into road vehicles. Windows midway along each of the shorter sides of the shed lit the main body of the shed and the small office.

The signal box was a neat, rectangular, timber-framed building with a gabled roof and matchboarded sides, lit by well proportioned multi-paned sliding windows facing the SDJR line and the up and down directions. This box and all the signalling equipment on the line was provided by the Worcester firm of Dutton & Co., incorporating a new pattern of interlocking frame designed by their Engineer, William Buck. In Buck's design, the device which held the levers in the normal or reverse positions was placed under the floor, rather than having a quadrant above the floor. The main lever was pivoted at the top and connected to a catch-rod which ran down the front of the lever. The action of pulling or pushing the lever locked or unlocked the catch mechanism. Only about 10 frames to this pattern are known and according to Buck in his unpublished memoirs, only about 400 of these levers were produced. Inside the Edington box, a Dutton Type 1,

Somerset & Dorset Joint Railway platform barrow of the Midland Type 210 design at Edington Junction. The BR fire-buckets show that this elderly barrow had survived into the post-Nationalisation era and outlived the Bridgwater Railway. The 'drinking water' churns show that the staff 'cuppas' were dependent on the train delivering this basic commodity.

D. Milton, Robin Atthill Collection, SDRT Archive

Somerset & Dorset Joint Railway luggage barrow. This single-wheel variety was also photographed at Edington Junction. A similar one was measured by A.E. West at Sturminster Newton in 1965 and drawn by D.B.R. Grist for the South-Western Circle (ref. no. SWC/M/4).

D. Milton, Robin Atthill Collection, SDRT Archive

there was a 35-lever frame and Buck's photograph on page 42 shows it with
the usual furnishings comprising several block instruments, a chair, a desk,
a stove and an oil lamp. At a later date, certainly by 1913, the Dutton frame
had been replaced by a 39-lever Stevens frame.

Trains leaving Edington Junction passed milepost 0 and veered south-
west past the home signal followed by the distant signal for trains
approaching Edington Junction from Bridgwater. The line curved on an
embankment towards Chilton Drove crossing and then over the old Glastonbury Canal, straightening out before milepost 1, continuing past Stone End
Crossing and New Close Drove where the embankment ended and a short
cutting began. The railway then began to curve towards the west, rising on
an embankment over Dole Lane past milepost 2, into a cutting under Land-
shire Lane until it straightened out on the level adjacent to Board's Quarry
which was served by a single siding and short headshunt. This was controlled by a 3-lever ground-frame, released by the tablet, which controlled the
facing point lock, points, a bolt on the siding gate and shunt signals for
movements in and out of the siding. After continuing west for a short length,
the line curved towards the south through a cutting, under a road bridge and
into Cossington Station.

Although there was just one platform on the south side of the line,
Cossington station buildings were the most imposing on the Bridgwater
Railway. Built of limestone, the two storey station master's house adjoined
the single storey station offices of ladies waiting room, booking office and
general waiting room, station master's office, goods office and conveniences.
A comparison of the contractor's drawings with photographic evidence
shows that extra windows were incorporated when built, lighting the up-
stairs landing and main bedroom on the platform side and the hall and
cupboard on the ground floor. Despite being provided with a substantial
three-bedroomed house with sitting room, kitchen, scullery and W.C., no
bathroom was provided. As in thousands of homes across the country,
bathing took place in a galvanised zinc tub placed in front of the kitchen
range and filled by precariously lifting utensils of hot water from the range
and tipping their contents into the bath.

On the platform there was a simple pitched roof awning projecting from
the station offices and supported on four upright pillars. A short loop was
provided on the Bridgwater side of the station to facilitate shunting of the
single goods siding. The loop also served a head shunt for the siding. The
four points serving Cossington, with the associated signals, were operated
from a ground-frame hut situated on the platform, close to the station
master's house. The hut was a simple timber-framed, weather-boarded structure with a pitched roof and two 6-paned windows facing up and down
directions. Outside was hung the SDJR oval electric-telegraph board which,
if it showed its white face with a blue cross, indicated that the system was in
working order.

This hut was similar to one in Dutton's catalogue described as a 'standard
ground-frame hut', surviving today as 'Cranmore West GF' on the East
Somerset Railway. In 1890 it contained an 8-lever frame, but in 1896, when

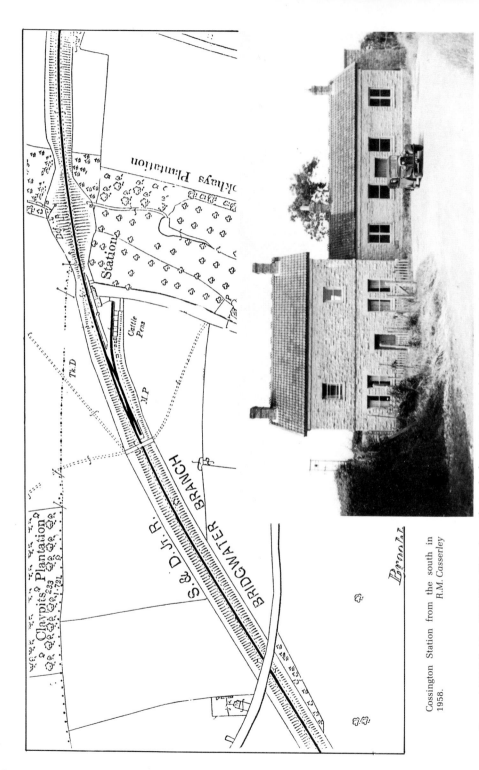

Cossington Station from the south in 1958.
R.M. Casserley

Somerset 25" O.S. Map Ll.5(1902). This shows the track plan at Cossington dating from 1896 when the pointwork was modified so that goods trains could be shunted from either direction.
Courtesy Ordnance Survey

These drawings of Cossington Station show the buildings and the ground-frame hut as built.

Drawings by John Childs

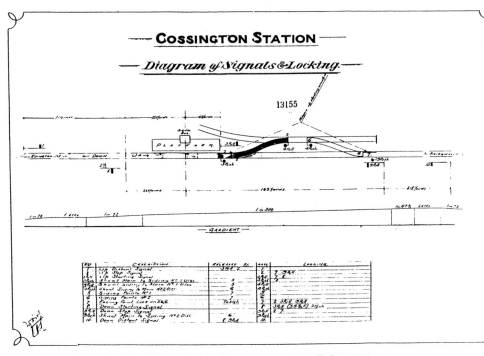

Cossington signalling diagram showing the arrangements installed in 1896.
Reproduced by courtesy of the Public Record Office, Kew

Cossington signalling diagram showing the simplified layout after 1933.
Drawing by Chris Osment

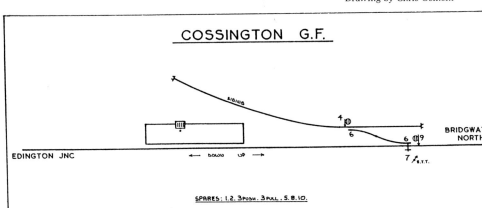

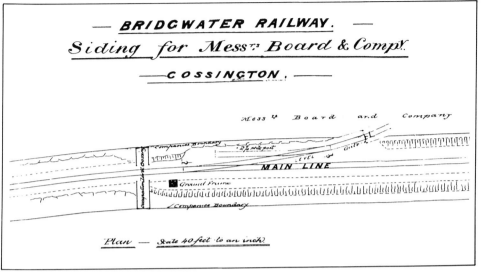

Plan of the arrangements for Board's Siding.
Reproduced by courtesy of the Public Record Office, Kew

BOARD'S SIDING between COSSINGTON and EDINGTON JUNCTION.

The Points of this Siding lie towards Edington Junction, and they are released by the Train Tablet for the Section, in accordance with Rule 34 of the Electric Train Tablet Block Regulations.

This Siding may be worked by a train running from Bridgwater or Edington Junction.

When the Siding is worked from Edington Junction the wagons must be pushed in front of the Engine and there must be a Brake Van at the Bridgwater end of the train, and the train must not exceed a speed of 15 miles per hour, and the Driver must have in his possession a Tablet for the Section, which Tablet must in all cases be returned to Edington Junction. On reaching the Siding the train must be placed above the Siding Points with the Brake well secured, and any Wagon Brakes, and Sprags in addition that may be necessary, must be used to prevent the train from moving. When the Engine is detached, it will go into the Siding to fetch out the Loaded Wagons, the empties being afterwards placed in the Siding, and after the van is attached to the loaded wagons, the train must return to Edington Junction.

Extract from the Appendix to the Somerset & Dorset Joint Line Working Time-table, October 1909, Page 190, governing the operation of the Board's Quarry siding.

the existing siding point was moved a little in the Bridgwater direction, and an extra point inserted facing Edington to form a run-round loop just beyond the Bridgwater end of the platform, a 10-lever frame occupied the hut of which, according to the Board of Trade report, 'three are push/pull levers', while recommending that '3-push' & '9-push' and '3-push' & '4-pull' should be interlocked and adding that 'if the company wish to do so, the signals at Cossington may be removed'. At a later date the main running signals were removed and the point facing Edington was abolished around 1933. Alongside the siding was a row of cattle pens which reflected a major trade in this area. At the end of the siding there was a carriage loading dock. Other goods facilities included a loading gauge, a coal bin, a corrugated iron lamp room, a sawdust store, an ash pit and a gangers' hut.

Passing milepost 3 the line continued in its cutting, passed under three roadbridges before turning to the right and past milepost 4 into Bawdrip Halt. This had been built in 1923 in consequence of a 182-signature petition submitted to the Somerset & Dorset Railway which argued that there were about 300 people living there without the benefits of any shops. There was a bus service to Bridgwater, where Bawdrip people went to shop, but the buses were crowded, especially on market days. After a favourable engineering report a platform was provided and single fares set at 4½d. to Bridgwater, 1½d. to Cossington and 6d. to Edington Junction. The fares were to be collected by the guard on the train, the moneys being deposited with the booking offices of Edington or Bridgwater depending on the direction of travel. If a passenger wished to travel beyond Edington then he or she would be required to book again at that station. Excursions starting at Bawdrip would be provided with through tickets in advance, by prior arrangement with the station master at Bridgwater.

Having succeeded in obtaining a halt, the inhabitants of Bawdrip quickly followed up with a request for a shelter. George Wheeler, the S & D Joint line traffic superintendent, was agreeable to the request in the light of the traffic brought to the line by the new halt and approached the Engineer to provide plans and an estimate. A shelter built of concrete with asbestos roofing was estimated by the Engineer to cost £28.

After leaving the Halt en route to Bridgwater, trains crossed a stone bridge across the main north/south route in the village and continued at roof-top height on an embankment that descended to the level at the point where the line crossed the King's Sedgemoor Drain. From the Drain to milepost 5 there was a slight embankment, then the line was crossed by a bridge that carried the main Bridgwater to Glastonbury A39 road over the railway.

The next road crossing was at Horsey Lane, an unclassified road which connected Horsey Pill, Horsey, Manor Farm and Horsey Level with the A39. As this road was crossed on the level, crossing gates had to be provided and a lodge provided for the crossing keeper. The lodge was a single-storied structure of brick with a slate covered gabled roof. In the wall facing Horsey Lane were two elegant 12-paned sash windows that reached to the eaves and lit two rooms: the living room of 11 ft square and a bedroom of 10 ft × 11 ft. These two rooms were separated by an internal wall and chimney breast that provided a fireplace for both rooms, and facilitated the construction of

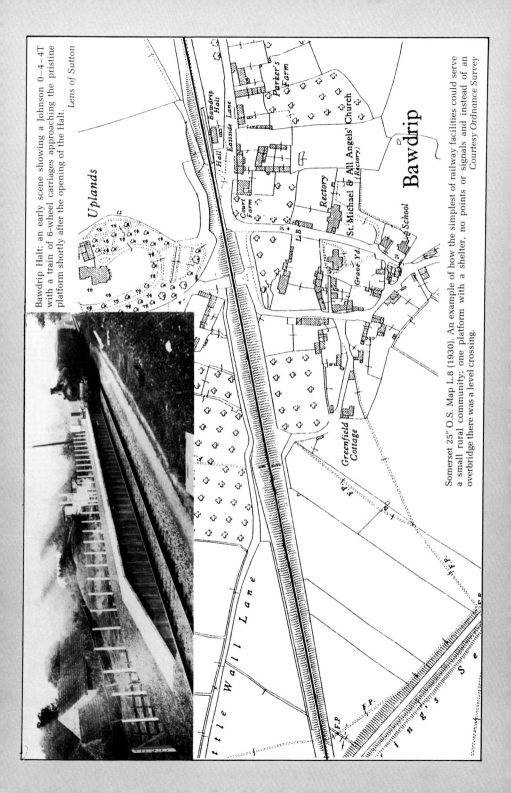

Bawdrip Halt; an early scene showing a Johnson 0–4–4T with a train of 6-wheel carriages approaching the pristine platform shortly after the opening of the Halt.

Lens of Sutton

Somerset 25″ O.S. Map L.8 (1930). An example of how the simplest of railway facilities could serve a small rural community; one platform with a shelter, no points or signals and instead of an overbridge there was a level crossing.

Courtesy Ordnance Survey

Uplands

Bawdrip

Parker's Farm

Bawdrip Hall

Hall

Eastside Lane

Court Farm

Rectory

St. Michael & All Angels' Church

(Rectory)

L.B

Grave Yd

School

Greenfield Cottage

ttle Wall Lane

F.P.

F.P.

F.P.

F.P.

Sedges

F.P.

King's

A Sunday School party at Bawdrip Halt in 1927 awaiting a train to Burnham-on-Sea via Edington Junction.   *W. Locke*

Bawdrip Halt with a close-up view of the shelter. The passengers have probably alighted from the train, having been shopping in Bridgwater.   *L & GRP Collection, courtesy David & Charles*

cupboards between the chimney breast and the back wall. From the living room the main external door was sheltered by a porch facing towards the railway. The gabled roof continued down, cats-claw fashion, at the rear to house the lean-to kitchen measuring 8 ft × 7 ft with a sink and a copper in opposite corners. At a healthy distance from the lodge a brick privy was provided with internal dimensions of 6 ft × 3 ft. The door left an 18-inch gap at the top for ventilation. The privy's rear sloping roof, having no gutter, dripped its rain water into an open ash-pit.

From Horsey Lane Crossing the line ascended an incline that took it past milepost 6 and over the GWR Bristol–Exeter line and the A38 road from Bridgwater to Bristol, from which point the Bridgwater Railway curved towards the south and descended to the level just past Kimberley Terrace. Opposite Kimberley Terrace a siding curved towards the River Parrett to serve the Spinx Cement Works, later known as Wilds Cement Works and afterwards as Board's Cement Works. Board's siding was controlled by a 3-lever ground-frame in similar fashion to the one controlling their quarry siding. Passing allotments to the left the line then passed over the Drove with its tramway leading to Colthurst and Symonds brickyard.

As the Drove was crossed on the level, another crossing lodge was provided together with an outside privy. From this point on it is interesting to compare the original contractor's drawings with the Ordnance Survey maps of 1904 and 1930 to see the variations between planning and building and later alterations to the layout at Bridgwater. The contractor's drawings show that the road known as The Leggar had to be diverted to join The Drove and what was left of it between the railway and the A38 road became known as Quantock Terrace. Just to the south of the crossing keeper's lodge, a turnout gave access to the run-round loop, the goods' sidings and the wharf, the main line continuing in a straight line to the arrival face of the island platform. The contractor's drawing shows the platform to have been 300 ft long between the north face of the station building and the top of the ramp slope. Apart from a short tapered portion, the platform was 50 ft wide. The awning, with its arc roof supported on pairs of columns, stretched 200 ft along the platform, although a short section between the main awning and the station building was filled in with a pitched roofed awning with its slope descending towards the station building.

The signal box, with thirteen levers, was originally situated about half-way between the two turn-outs that gave access to the run-round loop, on the east side of the main line. By 1930 the box had been moved to the other side of the main line opposite the crossing keeper's lodge, presumably for operational reasons but not to operate the crossing gates, because these were still worked by hand. This second box had a 14-lever frame of the 'knee' pattern favoured by the LSWR for use in ground level boxes.

It was envisaged that the goods yard sidings leading off the run-round loop would have a short head-shunt running parallel to the main line. This was altered to provide a head-shunt that ran up to The Leggar, with another turn-out provided to make a siding that would serve the coaling stage. Adjacent to the coaling stage siding was the line leading to the 50 ft turntable of South Western design and the 60 ft engine shed. The two sidings closest to the passenger roads were to have had a crossover at the southern end, but this does not appear to have been constructed. Of these two sidings, the one nearest to the departure track was used for coal wagons while the siding adjacent to it was for general merchandise.

Another feature that does not seem to have been built was a run-round loop for the goods shed. Instead one siding ran through the goods shed, while the siding immediately to the east, and fitted with a loading gauge, stopped short of it and was generally used for brick and tile traffic. The siding behind the goods shed was equipped with a weighing table but was frequently used for stabling empty wagons. A further siding ran to the corner of the goods yard site. This was equipped with a 5-ton crane that was occasionally used to lift bulk timber, although one doubts if the staff had much affection for it as it required four porters to operate it! The last siding served the cattle pens and crossed the Leggar to give access to the Wharf.

The station building was situated at the southern end of the platform with the ramp to the loading dock adjoining its western wall. Although of brick with a hipped and tiled roof, there was an option to build the walls in stone, according to the contractor's drawing. A comparison of the drawings with the photograph on page 61 shows that there were detail differences between what was planned and the structure that was actually built; the ticket office appears to have been given an extra window while one of the W.C.s has lost its window. A generous booking hall was flanked on the western side by the ticket office and the station master's office; on the eastern side lay the parcels room, the general waiting room, ladies waiting room, porters' room, stores and conveniences. The booking hall led out on to the station concourse, which was 20 ft deep and stretched from the departure platform face to the garden fence of the station master's house, giving access to an exit via a wicket gate at the front of the eastern side of the station building. Although the sash-windows at the side were rectangular with just two panes, the front ones had arched heads and four panes each.

The goods shed was designed to be built of brick or stone with internal measurements of 60 ft × 21 ft 6 in. The shed was lit on the track side by four 8-paned windows with shallow-arched lintels situated high in the wall. Access to the shed via the track could be barred by double wooden doors at each end. The internal platform was supported by the outer wall and by two brick piers that ran the whole length of the shed. A 2-ton crane was mounted on the platform to help unload some of the bulkier items from the wagons. In the platform wall, two loading bays were provided with large double doors. Pedestrian access to the platform could be by way of a set of steps to an end door at platform level, or by steps from track level inside the double-doors at each end. The roof was gabled with timber tie-beams, king-posts and braces.

By contrast, the engine shed sported an arched corrugated-iron roof reminiscent of the goods shed at Edington Junction. Its external dimensions were 60 ft × 25 ft and its brick walls were lit on each side by seven windows of eight panes each, the top pair being arched to match the lintels. The 14 ft doorways were set off-centre by 1 ft 6 in. An inspection pit was set beneath the track while the sleeper floor was laid on a 9 inch depth of ballast so that the top surface of the sleepers was level with the rails.

The siding, which continued past the cattle pens to give access to the wharf, crossed The Leggar and formed a passing loop served by a crane. This loop was at the apex of a sharp curve at the southern end of Castle Field, because to reach its wharf the Bridgwater Railway had to turn almost 180 degrees! At the western end of the loop a short spur led off to Barham's cement, lime, brick and tile works. The wharf line continued round the curve to serve a storage siding on the landward side of the wharf and then the wharf itself, with a run-round facility containing an additional crossover about a third of the way along the loop. The wharf itself was a substantial timber-framed structure that stretched for 400 ft along the east bank of the River Parrett. It comprised frames of four 14 inch piles each braced with timbers measuring 12 in. × 6 in. and the longest two piles were tied by an additional beam 12 inches square. These frames were set at 10 ft centres along the whole 400 ft length, tied to each other with 12 in. square beams and 9 in. square diagonals.

Set on top of the piles were lengths of 14 in. × 10 in. beams, to which were secured transverse planking, and then over the line of the 14 in. × 12 in. timbers were set further beams of 14 in. × 7 in. To these were attached rails set at 7 ft gauge for three travelling cranes, and, along the other pairs of piles, rails set at standard gauge for rolling stock. To protect the bank at the foot of the piles 6 inch sheet piling was driven in along the length of the wharf. Despite the size and complexity of the timber-work in this wharf, after 20 years much of it was so dilapidated that the wharf was removed and the sidings rationalised.

No.28A shunting the goods yard at Bridgwater in 1928 with the water tower and coaling-stage in the background.   J.E. Kite

Somerset 25″ O.S. Map L.11 (1904 and 1930 editions). These maps reveal detail differences such as:—
- the repositioning of the Bridgwater signal box from its original position by Quantock Terrace to The Drove Crossing
- Spinx Cement Works became Wild's Cement Works
- Re-alignment of the coaling stage siding
- Abandonment of much of the wharf and the rationalisation of the sidings.

The maps show the railway in its Bridgwater setting, revealing how close it was to the GWR, its position relative to several brick and tile manufacturers, the river and the dock complex on the other bank.

Courtesy Ordnance Survey

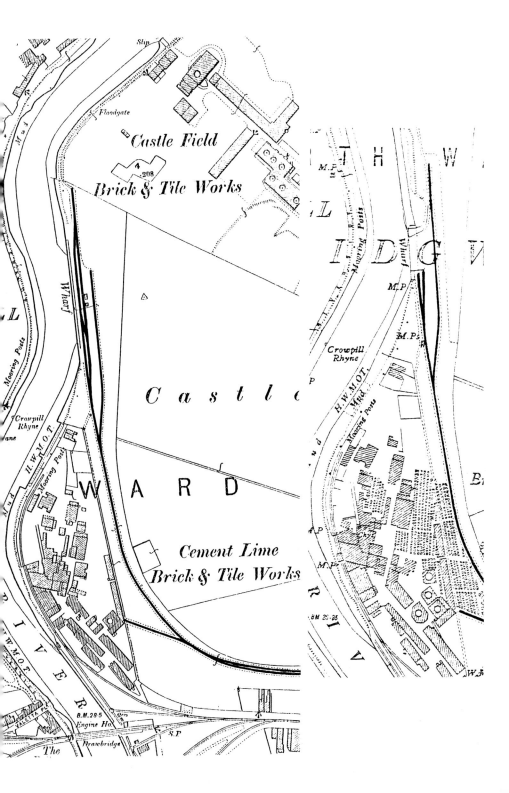

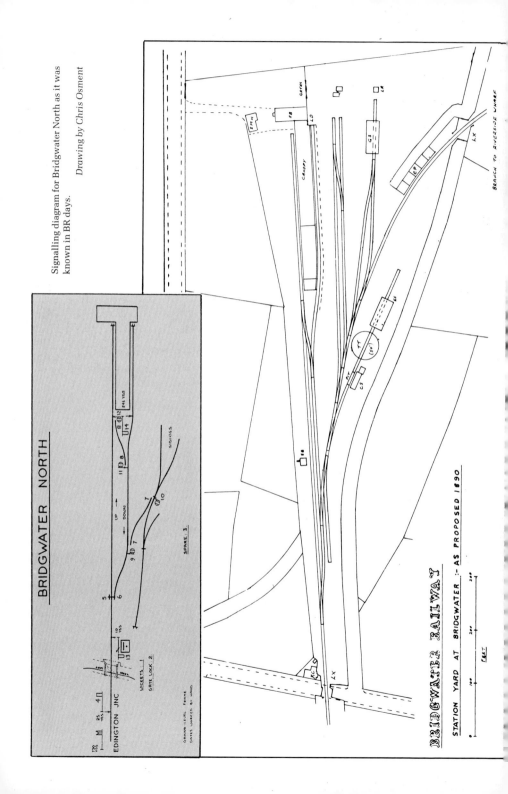

Signalling diagram for Bridgwater North as it was known in BR days.

Drawing by Chris Osment

Bridgwater: the station frontage. *L&GRP Collection, courtesy David & Charles*

The island platform at Bridgwater; the carriage is an SR one of LSWR origin.

L&GRP Collection, courtesy David & Charles

Bridgwater Station building as originally envisaged.

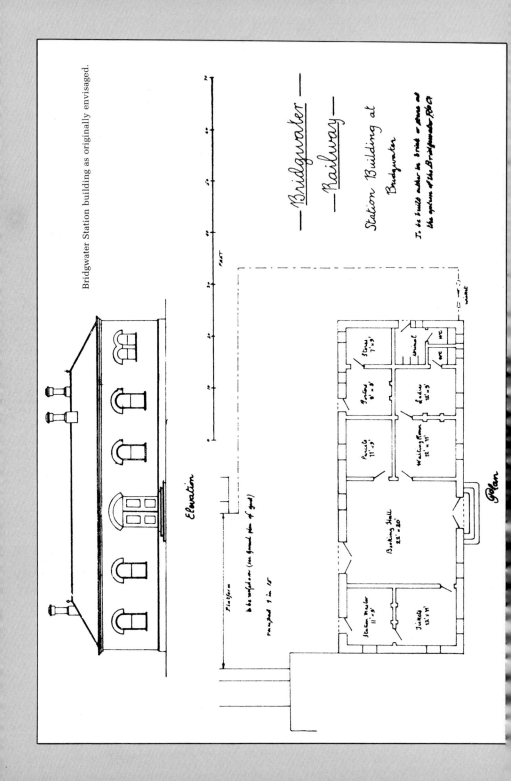

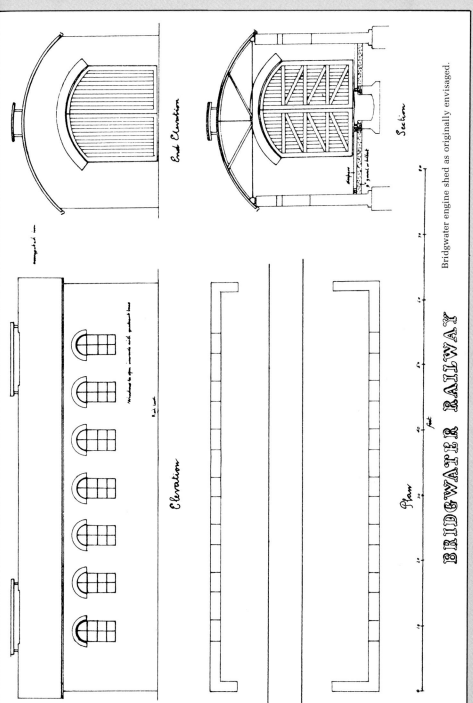

End Elevation

Section

Elevation

Plan

BRIDGWATER RAILWAY

Bridgwater engine shed as originally envisaged.

Drawing by Neil Pankhurst based on Contractors' drawing, courtesy of British Rail

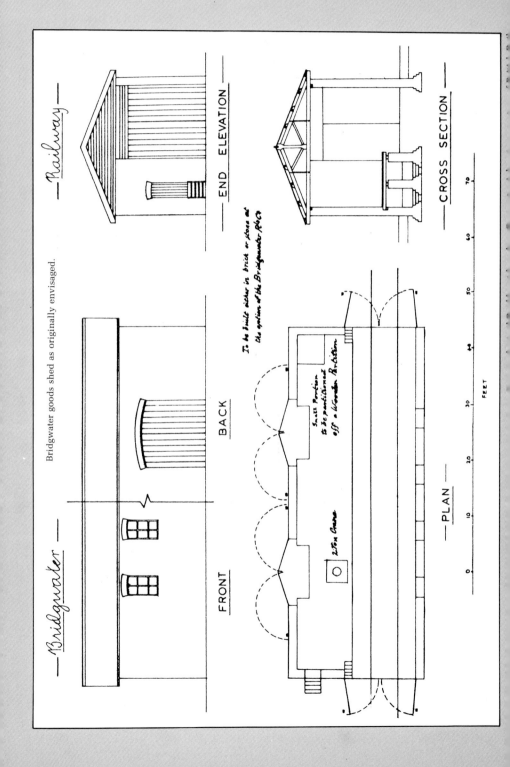

Bridgwater goods shed as originally envisaged.

Bridgwater — *Railway*

FRONT BACK — END ELEVATION —

To be built either in brick or stone at the option of the Bridgwater R/y C?

25Ton Crane

Small Portion to be partitioned off a Wooden Partition

— PLAN — CROSS SECTION —

0 10 20 30 40 50 60 70

FEET

Chapter Ten
Operations

Despite its nominal independence there was never much doubt that the Bridgwater Railway would be operated as part of the Somerset & Dorset Joint Railway system. The 7 mile line was never conceived as merely a railway from Bridgwater to the Somerset Levels; the lack of population and industry along its route would have ensured financial ruin. To run it purely as a rural railway would have been a negation of the driving forces that struggled for its construction for so long. By 1890, the case for giving Bridgwater a direct link with the standard gauge was all but dead, although the inconveniences of the Broad Gauge, real or imagined, had been influential in attracting support to the Bridgwater Railway. To break the GWR monopoly of transport in Bridgwater along with its perceived abuses was a major force behind the railway.

Perhaps even more important were the personalities of the railway interest outside Bridgwater that were harnessed to the cause. Bouverie, Reid and Toogood had expertise in creating railways in unrewarding financial climates; the Somerset & Dorset was a monument to that. Bridgwater gave them an opportunity to give the Somerset & Dorset access to one of the county's important towns and ports. The Bridgwater Railway seemed to have a momentum of its own, one in which Read and Toogood seemed to have been caught up, not just because they had been involved with the Somerset & Dorset since the 1850s, but because every time the idea of the Bridgwater Railway was mooted, they as General Manager and solicitor respectively were people capable of getting things done. They knew that the Somerset & Dorset did not have the resources to finance the line, but they did know how to entice capital for small lines that, in effect, would increase their network. Added to this was a sense of rivalry and competition and a continuance of their natural line of work. To give Bridgwater a link with Southampton and London via the South Western, and the industrial heartlands via the Midland, it would have been ludicrous to operate the line as an independent entity. It had to be worked as part of the Somerset & Dorset system.

The SDJR in taking over the operating lease from the LSWR realised that an attractive service would have to be operated to win traffic from the GWR in Bridgwater. In the opening year the entries in *Bradshaw* were arranged to show the Bridgwater Railway as the SDJR chief branch, taking precedence over Highbridge, Burnham and Wells. Publicity was given to two fast trains which ran between Bridgwater and Templecombe to connect with LSWR expresses to Waterloo. The distance of 35 miles could be covered in 66 minutes with stops at Edington and Glastonbury. The opening of the Bridgwater Railway coincided with an increase in Somerset & Dorset traffic and led to 25 new carriages being ordered. Until these were delivered the LSWR lent carriages to operate the Bridgwater Railway.

The Working Timetable for May 1892 reveals nine trains each way on the Bridgwater Railway. The first passenger train to arrive in Bridgwater was the 8.17 am, which had left Wells 47 minutes previously. There were two ordinary passenger trains from Evercreech, two from Templecombe and

SOMERSET & DORSET JOINT RAILWAY WORKING TIMETABLE, MAY 1892

UP	Goods Templecombe to Bridgwater and Highbridge	Pass. Wells to Bridgwater and Burnham	Pass. Evercreech to Bridgwater and Burnham	Pass. Templecombe to Bridgwater and Burnham	Fast Pass.* Templecombe to Bridgwater	Pass. Templecombe to Bridgwater and Burnham	Pass. Evercreech to Bridgwater	Pass. Wells to Bridgwater	Fast Pass. Templecombe to Bridgwater and Burnham
	am	am	am	pm	pm	pm	pm	pm	pm
Templecombe	4.20	—	—	12.15	1.52	3.08	—	—	8.15
Evercreech	5.55	—	10.25	12.47	2.12	3.33	4.50	—	8.33
Wells	—	7.30	—	—	—	—	—	7.30	—
Edington	7.43	8.05	11.14	1.34	2.45	14.15	5.47	8.07	9.15
Cossington	—	8.11	11.20	1.40	—	4.21	5.53	8.13	H9.20
Bridgwater	8.00	8.17	11.27	1.46	2.58	4.28	6.00	8.20	9.27

I This train will convey goods traffic from Edington to Bridgwater when required.

H Stops to set down passengers booked from stations beyond Evercreech.

* Local horse box and carriage traffic will not be conveyed by this train.

DOWN	Pass. Highbridge and Bridgwater to Evercreech	Fast Pass. Burnham and Bridgwater to Templecombe	Pass. Burnham and Bridgwater to Templecombe	Pass. Bridgwater to Evercreech	Goods and Empty Coaches Bridgwater to Edington	Fast Pass. Burnham and Bridgwater to Templecombe	Goods Bridgwater to Templecombe	Pass. Burnham and Bridgwater to Wells	Goods and Empty Coaches Bridgwater to Edington
	am	am	pm	pm	pm	pm	pm	pm	pm
Bridgwater	7.10	10.20	12.10	3.25	3.40	K6.10	7.00	8.45	9.40
Cossington	7.17	G10.27	12.16	3.31	3.50	6.16	B	8.52	—
Edington	7.22	10.32	12.22	3.37	4.05	6.22	7.18	9.00	9.55
Wells	—	—	—	—	—	—	—	9.55	—
Evercreech	8.19	11.11	1.30	4.27	—	7.00	8.47	—	—
Templecombe	—	11.28	1.55	—	—	7.16	10.07	—	—

K This train will stop at Shapwick, Ashcott, West Pennard, Pylle, Evercreech Jnc., Cole and Wincanton to set down passengers booked from Bridgwater and Cossington only.

B Stops at Cossington when required to pick up market traffic.

G Stops by signal to pick up through passengers only.

ALL ENGINES NOT RUNNING FUNNEL FIRST MUST STOP AT COSSINGTON WHETHER MARKED TO DO SO OR NOT.

another one from Wells. Two fast passenger trains from Templecombe did the journey in 1 hour 6 minutes compared with 1 hour 20 minutes and 1 hour 31 minutes for the ordinary passenger trains. There was one up goods each day arriving at 8.00 am; this had left Templecombe at 4.20. Down trains comprised two passenger trains to Evercreech, two fast passenger trains to Templecombe, two goods and empty coaches to Edington, one goods train to Templecombe and one passenger train to Wells.

In anticipation of the extra traffic to be handled, the Somerset & Dorset converted one of its Fox Walker saddle tanks, No.8, into a side tank with 4ft 6in. wheels to work goods and passenger services over the Bridgwater and Wells branches. Although the engine's appearance was altered significantly, it was still an attractive locomotive in its new guise and similar to the standard MR goods tank. Presumably the traffic on the Bridgwater branch did not justify its use for long. No photographic evidence has come to light showing No.8 on the branch, and it seems that more useful employment was found for it on the steeper gradients of the main Bath–Bournemouth line.

By the early years of the 20th century an additional morning train between Bridgwater and Edington was laid on to meet a Highbridge–Templecombe train. However, the grand service of 1892 was never to be surpassed, and, despite the years 1890–1914 being a golden age for the SDJR, the traffic on the Bridgwater Railway lived up to its critics' prophecies. Thus by 1914 the services had been reduced to six trains a day in each direction. The fast passenger trains had been dropped and the motive power seen on the line featured comparative lightweights, such as the George England rebuilds, 2–4–0Ts Nos.27A and 28A.

JULY–SEPTEMBER 1903 TIMETABLE

	am	am	HC am	noon	pm	pm	pm	
Bridgwater	6.50	8.55	10.00	12.00	3.30	4.55	8.20	
Cossington	6.57	9.01	10.06	12.06	3.36	5.03	8.27	
Edington Jn	7.02	9.07	10.12	12.12	3.42	5.10	8.33	
	am	am	am	pm	pm	pm	pm	pm
Edington Jn	8.00	9.15	11.15	1.27	2.52	5.54	8.40	10.02
Cossington	8.06	9.21	11.21	1.33	2.58	6.00	8.46	10.08
Bridgwater	8.12	9.27	11.28	1.39	3.05	6.07	8.52	10.14

HC = Horses and private carriages are not conveyed by this train except by special arrangement under exceptional circumstances.

The emphasis given to fast links to Templecombe may have been good for publicity in the opening years, but the line was not being operated only for the sake of two prestigious passenger trains a day in each direction. As well as freight traffic, local passenger traffic had to be considered even though the demand might be modest. The 'Regulation of Railways Act' of 1889 gave the opportunity to obtain permission to operate Mixed Trains, that is trains consisting of both passenger and goods vehicles. This gave railways operating in rural districts an opportunity to economise where traffic was meagre

Rebuilt Fox-Walker 0−6−0T No.8. Was this the 'powerful side tank for the Bridgwater Branch'?
L&GRP Collection, courtesy David & Charles

No.38 (formerly No.61) sporting a G5 boiler and Belpaire firebox as rebuilt in March 1928.
L&GRP Collection, courtesy David & Charles

No.74 built 1902. These were larger and more powerful than the 'Scotties'.
L&GRP Collection, courtesy David & Charles

and speeds low. Early in 1891, the SDJR applied to the Board of Trade for permission to operate 22 of its services as mixed trains, of which the following were on the Bridgwater branch:

11.14 am Edington–Bridgwater
4.15 pm Edington–Bridgwater
5.47 pm Edington–Bridgwater
7.20 am Bridgwater–Edington
3.25 pm Bridgwater–Evercreech

Such trains were a familiar feature on the Bridgwater Railway up until its final years, as the photographs on pages 8 and 70–74 show.

As with other railways, operations were subject to a variety of bye-laws. There were penalties for travelling without a valid ticket; males over, or apparently over, the age of eight were prohibited from travelling in compartments reserved for female passengers 'except by the express permission of the guard'. There were bye-laws against intoxication, bad language, travelling on roofs, on footboards or in luggage compartments. Animals were prohibited from compartments; weapons were also banned, as was vandalism, selling on railway property or its approaches, betting, throwing objects from windows and spitting in all its foul forms. These are among the more colourful examples among a set of regulations that make tedious reading and set onerous responsibilities on railway staff to such an extent that many must have been difficult, if not impractical, to enforce.

The early years of the 20th century witnessed an experiment on the Bridgwater Railway which was to have a significant effect on the SDJR and other railways with single lines. The locomotive superintendent of the SDJR, Alfred Whittaker, had devised an apparatus that enabled single line tablets to be exchanged whilst in motion thus speeding up train services. Whitaker's system used the Bridgwater line as its proving ground. Once it was accepted, the whole line from Edington to Bridgwater was designated as one section, i.e. only one train could travel on the line at a time.

Before a train could commence its journey the crew had to have in their possession the section's tablet, in this case a round tablet with a round central hole and a semi-spherical notch in the perimeter. The tablet would be given up at Edington or Bridgwater to enable another train to travel over the section. Those trains that only worked as far as Board's quarry drew the tablet according to special regulations that enabled the train to work the quarry siding, where the tablet was used to unlock the frame. The tablet was then returned and the line cleared. Despite being tried out on the Bridgwater branch, Whittaker's apparatus was only used in service on the Bath–Bournemouth section.

When approached from Edington, Board's siding had to be worked according to instructions laid down in the working timetable. The train had to be propelled backwards at no more than 15 mph and placed above the siding. The brakes on the brake van and trucks then had to be secured, after which the engine could be uncoupled and go into the siding to fetch out the loaded wagons, the empties afterwards being placed in the siding.

On 5th September, 1952, H.C. Casserley took a series of photographs on the Bridgwater Railway that relate the tale of a mixed train; the 1.40 pm from Bridgwater to Edington Junction. In this view we see three carriages parked alongside the departure platform. *H.C. Casserley*

Moving onto the island platform Casserley has taken this view showing the arrival platform clear up to the buffer stops and the MCC-blazered 'Brylcream' advert on the station building. Note the trucks in the siding on the right. *H.C. Casserley*

A Johnson 0-4-4T No. 58072 pulls the trucks out of the siding . . .   *H.C. Casserley*

. . . and shunts them back alongside the arrival platform.   *H.C. Casserley*

No. 58072 then left the trucks by the arrival platform and reversed back to couple up to the carriages.   *H.C. Casserley*

With a good head of steam, No. 58072 is ready to depart with the 1.40 pm to Edington, but first it has to pick up the trucks in the arrival platform.   *H.C. Casserley*

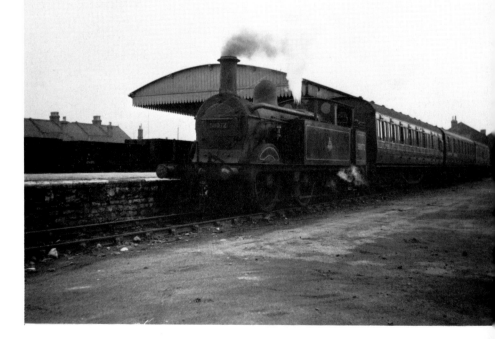

No. 58072 climbs Cossington bank with the 1.40 pm ex-Bridgwater . . .   *H.C. Casserley*

. . . and as it trundles through Cossington station we can get a better idea of the length of this mixed train.   *H.C. Casserley*

Another view of the mixed train as it rounds the curve by the Bridgwater siding into Edington.

H.C. Casserley

... and comes to a rest by the down main platform at Edington Junction.   *H.C. Casserley*

This steam crane built by Thomas Smith of Rodley, near Leeds, ran on broad gauge track, transferring goods between ships and trucks at Bridgwater wharf. *British Rail*

SDJR 6-wheeled 3rd class saloon No.89. This vehicle had seats for 32 people. The SDJR contemplated such a saloon for Bridgwater passenger traffic in 1923 as it would carry all the anticipated traffic except in the height of summer. *Oakwood Collection*

Rebuilt George England 2−4−0T No.28A, which lost a spring at Cossington in the 1920s while crossing the points.   *Authors Collection*

No.28A in an earlier guise as a saddle tank.   *L&GRP Collection, courtesy David & Charles*

There were also special instructions for Bridgwater. Drivers were informed that Bridgwater was a dead-end station and that they must not assume that the lines were clear up to the stop blocks as vehicles would frequently be standing at the platform. To work the wharf, trains and engines had to be in the charge of an authorised shunter. As the level crossing gates by the cattle dock were locked, engines had to stop while the shunter unlocked the gates, signalled the driver to proceed and then closed and locked the gates.

The problem of lack of passenger traffic on the SDJR branches led the traffic superintendent to suggest in January 1906 that 'Motor cars with an engine strong enough to pull two trailers would be adequate for the Bridgwater and Wells branches'. This would save two engines and four ordinary carriages yielding savings of £450 p.a. The Joint Committee was impressed with this idea and instructed that orders be placed for two motor cars at £4,000 each. By late April the order was cancelled as the Joint Committee by then considered that the motor cars were too expensive in relation to the estimated savings. Meanwhile the LSWR offered the loan of an 'H12' class steam railcar for trials. This railcar could carry 40 passengers and a small amount of luggage. Such a capacity was adequate for normal working but at times such as market days it could not cope. When a 6-wheeled carriage was added for the surplus passengers the railcar was unable to pull its load. Even on its own it had steaming difficulties, so the railcar was returned and the Bridgwater Railway resumed conventional operating.

Conventional working meant three or four 6-wheeled carriages, or perhaps two bogie vehicles, pulled by a Johnson 0–4–4T. Avonside No. 32 was photographed at Bridgwater in 1905. Vulcans Nos. 52 and 53 were recorded as being allocated to Bridgwater at one time. Goods trains were probably handled by the SDJR 0–6–0's, usually 'Scotties', sometimes a Fowler and occasionally a 'Bulldog'. However, the 0–4–4T engines, although referred to as passenger engines, could also haul goods trains. A loading table set out the maximum number of wagons that engines were permitted to haul:

Locomotive Type	Mineral wagons	Others
0–4–4T	16	35
Scotties (Nielson)	20	35
Fox Walkers	23	40
Scotties (Vulcan)	23	40
Fowlers	28	49
Bulldogs	28	49

By 1920 the engines were referred to by power classification and the working timetable showed this revision of wagon loading over the Bridgwater branch:

Power Class	Minerals	Goods	Empties
No.1 class (0–4–4T & Scotties)	19	25	34
No.2 class (Fowlers & Bulldogs)	20	27	36
No.3 class (Fox Wkr & 'G7' Bulldogs)	22	30	40

After the Great War there were no fast passenger services from Bridgwater and any illusions of it having been the senior branch had long gone. The

LSWR steam railcar No.2 of the same type as No.1, which was tried experimentally on the Bridgwater Railway to economise in running costs; seen here at Turnchapel *c.*1905.

D.A. Thompson Collection

SDJR Avonside 0−4−4T No.32 by the turntable at Bridgwater.

Robin Atthill Collection, SDRT Archive

OCTOBER 1920 TIMETABLE

	T'mbe	Bnmth SP	T'mbe	T'mbe	Ev'ch	Ev'ch A	Wells
	am	am	am	noon	pm	pm	pm
Bridgwater	6.40	7.40	9.10	12.00	3.00	4.55	8.25
Cossington	6.47	7.47	9.17	12.07	3.07	5.02	8.32
Edington Jn	6.54	7.54	9.24	12.14	3.14	5.09	8.39

SP = Excursion; runs to Bournemouth when required
A = Milk and perishables sent by this train and transferred at Edington

	Wells	Ev'ch	T'mbe	Ev'ch	Wells	Ev'ch
	am	am	pm	pm	pm	pm
Edington Jn	8.01	11.15	1.20	5.40	9.30	10.19
Cossington	8.07	11.21	1.26	5.47	9.36	10.25
Bridgwater	8.15	11.29	1.34	5.54	9.44	10.33

GOODS TRAINS

	Ev'ch B	Ed'n E	Ev'ch C D	Ed'n A
	pm	pm	pm	pm
Bridgwater	2.00	7.00	7.20	9.55
Edington Jn	2.20	7.20	7.40	10.07

A = Empty train
B = Runs only when specially advised. Engine and van must return Edington to Bridgwater immediately.
C = Stops at Cossington on Saturdays if required for cattle traffic.
D = Road Box No.42 for stations to Wimborne and Road Box No.43 for stations to Templecombe travel by this train.
E = Runs when required and for not less than 6 wagons.

	Ev'ch	T'mbe B	Ed'n C
	am	pm	pm
Edington Jn	8.40	3.50	7.25
Cossington		3.59	
Bridgwater	9.00	4.20	7.32

B = Goods, empty milk cans and Road boxes: No.1 from Bristol, No.6 from Bath, No.25 from London and No.35 from Wimborne
C = Engine and Van. Runs only when 7 pm Bridgwater–Edington runs*

*It would have been impossible for this engine and van to leave at 7.25 pm and for the 7.20 pm ex-Bridgwater to run at that time, but this is exactly as shown in the timetable. I suspect that when the 7 pm goods ex-Bridgwater ran, and its engine and van returned at 7.25 pm, the 7.20 pm goods ex-Bridgwater would have been retarded to about 7.35 pm.

Working Timetable for 1920 shows that there were just six passenger trains in each direction, with provision for an excursion train to Bournemouth when necessary. These trains were now allowed 14 minutes compared with the 12 minutes of 1892 and 1903. There were two goods trains in each direction, with provision for an extra one from Bridgwater if necessary, and balancing runs by engines and empty stock. The timing of the down goods trains within 20 minutes of each other was to cope with surges in traffic, the earlier one only running if the goods traffic that evening exceeded the permitted loading of the engine by six or more wagons. The timing of the arrivals at Edington were such that they were in advance of an equivalent train from Highbridge or Burnham, suggesting that passengers then had time to disembark at the bay platform and cross to the down platform to catch the train from Highbridge. Alternatively, the Bridgwater engine would have a little time in which to run round its carriages and propel them to the rear of the train from Highbridge when it arrived at the down platform.

Two years later the passenger timetable for July 1922 shows that the passenger service had increased to nine trains a day in each direction, plus a tenth on Wednesdays. This may have represented an increase in frequency for the summer months, and, although this was to be welcomed, economies in working were soon being sought. The following year it was calculated that a single saloon carrying 30 passengers would accommodate Bridgwater traffic except in the height of summer. It was estimated that the cost of fitting a third class saloon for the purpose would be £65. It is possible that the SDJR used one of their 3rd saloons Nos. 89, or 108 for the Bridgwater service. Both of these seated 32 passengers and each had a lavatory compartment, but the fact that alterations would have been needed to these vehicles suggests that other vehicles were used. Saloon No.6 was a first-class carriage carrying 26 passengers. This was not downgraded until 1928 so it seems possible that some other vehicle was converted to a saloon. Unfortunately no photographic evidence has come to light. Even if one of these saloons did work the Bridgwater branch, it could not have operated for more than nine years as they were withdrawn in 1932.

From 1928 push-pull trains were run on the line. This was the final development of the economy workings that had begun with the trials of the rail-cars in 1906. Johnson 0–4–4T's Nos. 30A, 31A, 32, 54 and 55 were fitted with the LMS vacuum system of motor train control and were used to operate the Wells, Burnham and Bridgwater sections. Only No. 32 survived longer than 1932. In 1930 the SDJR coaching stock had been shared out between the SR and LMS which by the end of 1946 had withdrawn all the old SDJR passenger vehicles from service. Photographic evidence indicates a return to conventional trains hauled by Johnson 0–4–4T's and LMS '3F' 0–6–0s.

By 1929 the extra market day train only ran from Edington to Bridgwater, presumably there were sufficient normal services to cope with the return traffic. The 1929 timetable also shows the effect on times of the opening of the Halt at Bawdrip, the overall journey now taking 16 minutes.

JULY 1922 TIMETABLE

	am	W am	am	am	am	pm	pm	pm	pm	pm
Bridgwater	6.35	8.30	9.30	10.40	11.45	3.10	5.10	6.30	8.30	9.30
Cossington	6.45	8.38	9.38	10.48	11.53	3.18	5.18	6.38	8.38	9.38
Edington Jn	6.49	8.44	9.44	10.54	11.59	3.24	5.24	6.44	8.45	9.44

	am	W am	am	am	pm	pm	pm	pm	pm	pm
Edington Jn	8.01	9.00	9.52	11.02	1.25	3.37	5.40	7.20	8.55	9.55
Cossington	8.08	9.07	9.59	11.09	1.32	3.44	5.47	7.27	9.02	10.02
Bridgwater	8.15	9.14	10.06	11.16	1.39	3.51	5.54	7.34	9.09	10.09

W = Wednesdays only

SEPTEMBER 1929 TIMETABLE

	am	am	am	pm	pm	pm	pm	pm
Bridgwater	8.05	9.50	11.20	1.10	3.05	5.10	6.30	8.15
Bawdrip	8.10	9.55	11.25	1.15	3.10	5.15	6.35	8.20
Cossington	8.14	9.59	11.29	1.19	3.14	5.19	6.39	8.24
Edington Jn	8.21	10.06	11.36	1.26	3.21	5.26	6.46	8.31

	am	am	D am	am	pm	pm	pm	pm	pm	pm
Edington Jn	7.38	8.30	9.10	10.55	12.30	1.35	4.42	5.40	7.15	9.00
Cossington		8.36		11.01	12.36	1.41	4.48	5.46	7.21	9.06
Bawdrip Halt		8.40		11.05	12.40	1.45	4.52	5.50	7.25	9.10
Bridgwater	7.53	8.46	9.25	11.11	12.46	1.51	4.58	5.56	7.31	9.16

D = Wednesday only

The Passenger and Milk Train timetable of 1931 shows only a few changes from the service of 1929, but the footnotes emphasise the restricted nature of the Bridgwater service. The 5.40 pm from Edington ran only on Wednesdays as a mixed train while the 10.55 am and 12.30 pm services could also be mixed. The 9.10 am from Edington would only stop at Cossington if necessary, while the 8.25 am to Wells and the 5.40 pm from Edington were to be 'formed of the Southern Brake Third usually kept at Edington', with a seating capacity of 30, interestingly identical to the proposed saloon conversion of 1923.

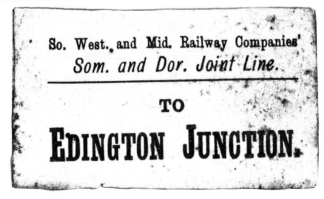

So. West., and Mid. Railway Companies'
Som. and Dor. Joint Line.

TO

EDINGTON JUNCTION.

SEPTEMBER 1931 TIMETABLE

	Wells	T'mbe	T'mbe		A		B	Wells C
	am	am	am	pm	pm	pm	pm	pm
Bridgwater	8.05	9.50	11.25	1.10	3.05	5.10	6.30	8.25
Bawdrip Halt	8.10	9.55	11.30	1.15	3.10	5.15	6.35	8.30
Cossington	8.14	9.59	11.34	1.19	3.14	5.19	6.39	8.34
Edington Jn	8.21	10.06	11.41	1.26	3.21	5.26	6.46	8.41

A = Traffic from Bridgwater branch must be sent down by this train to connect with the 4.40 from Edington.

B = After arrival at Edington will leave empty for Highbridge at 7.15.

C = This train to be formed of Southern Brake Third usually stationed at Edington.

	Wells D		E				T'mbe	T'mbe	F
	am	am	am	am	pm	pm	pm	pm	pm	pm
Edington Jn	7.38	8.30	9.10		10.55	12.30	1.35	4.42	5.40	9.00
Cossington		8.36			11.11	12.36	1.41	4.48	5.46	9.06
Bawdrip Halt		8.40			11.05	12.40	1.45	4.52	5.50	9.10
Bridgwater	7.53	8.46	9.25		11.11	12.46	1.51	4.58	5.56	9.16

D = May stop at Cossington to set down passengers when necessary, Edington Jn to advise driver. Train ex Wells.

E = Wednesdays only as a mixed train. The 10.55 and 12.30 may also run as mixed trains on Wednesday if necessary.

F = Formed of Southern Brake Third usually kept at Edington J.

EMPTY TRAIN	pm	
Bridgwater	9.50	This runs when required.
Edington Jn	10.05	

In the museum of the Somerset & Dorset Railway Trust at Washford there is a poster advertising a series of excursion trains laid on in 1930 to bring people to the Bridgwater Flower Show and Band Festival. Excursions such as this enabled the Bridgwater Railway to bloom because they demonstrated the scale of traffic that the railway was capable of handling. Three special trains plus the offer of reduced fares showed that the railway was touting for business. Unfortunately we do not know how large the trains were or the numbers they carried on that day, or if these excursions were no more than re-scheduled service trains. Nevertheless, it was an occasion showing the railway at its best, as on other occasions such as the spectacular winter carnival and St Matthew's Fair in Bridgwater. These events attracted excursions from as far away as Bath, consisting of 12 coaches double-headed over the Poldens.

Will Locke remembered one such event in 1947 when a 10-corridor-coach train was double-headed by two 'Bulldogs'; five of the coaches were stored in the arrival platform and five in the departure platform. Meanwhile the scheduled services had extra carriages attached to them to cope with the local demand. On its opening day, the Fair could bring over a thousand passengers on to the Bridgwater Railway. Excursion traffic was also brought

An excursion about to depart from Bridgwater *c.*1910 *en route* for Blackpool, carrying the Bridgwater Allotments Association in 11 Midland Railway clerestory coaches. Driver Frank Braund is on the footplate, station master Hawkins is standing on the right.

J. Townroe, Robin Atthill Collection, SDRT Archive

The return of the Blackpool excursion, hauled by SDJR rebuilt Fowler 0–6–0 No.22.

R. Fitzhugh Collection

At first I thought this was a group of excursionists but the presence of the sergeant and a few others in uniform suggests that this view c.1914 is of a group of young men prior to their departure to a training camp, followed by Flanders. *R. Fitzhugh Collection*

The former goods shed at Bridgwater. *W. Locke*

to the railway by various clubs, such as the Bridgwater Allotment Association, and some employers like the brick and tile manufacturers, Colthurst Symonds, who arranged trips for their workers from Bridgwater to Blackpool and Southsea.

Bridgwater Flower Show
& Band Festival
in the
Blake Gardens, Bridgwater
Process, of Bands @ 1.30

The Largest & Best of its Kind
in the West of England.

On Saturday, August 18th

Half-Day Excursions
will run to
Bridgwater

From	Depart	Depart	Depart	3rd class Fares
Wells	11.55	1.00	3.35	1/6
Polsham	12.03	1.05	3.41	1/6
Glastonbury	12.10	1.15	4.14	1/3
Ashcott	12.21	1.22	4.21	1/3
Shapwick	12.26	1.26	4.26	1/-
Edington	12.32	1.35	4.35	10d.
Cossington	12.41	1.41	4.41	7d.
Bawdrip	12.47	1.45	4.45	5d.
Bridgwater Arr	12.53	1.51	4.51	

The return train leaves Bridgwater at 10.00 pm the same day.

Cheap-day return tickets available from all stations within rail distance of 60 miles.

The passenger timetables for July–September 1939 and May 1945 illustrate the changed circumstances occasioned by World War II. The 1945 timetable shows that down trains had been halved in number and up trains were reduced from eight to five, compared with July 1939. Journey times by 1945 had now lengthened to 22 minutes. During the war there were numerous troop movements over the line and, as seen at stations all over Britain, there were many tearful farewells and joyous welcomes. Poignant memories were recalled by Mrs D. Gardner quoted by the *Western Daily Press* when the branch was finally closed; she remembered that after her husband had been home on leave, her small son and herself would accompany him as far as Edington, where 'there was an engine driver who was always on duty at the same time. He did not know us but when we got to Edington he had to turn the engine round to come back. He would say to us, "See your husband off my dear, we will wait a few minutes for you", and he always waited.' It is possible that the driver was driving a Southern engine at the time because six ex-LSWR 'T1' class 0–4–4Ts were allocated to Templecombe and Highbridge during the war and it is highly likely that they were used to work the Bridgwater branch.

Avonside No.31A fitted for push-pull working of the Wells and Bridgwater branches.

L&GRP Collection, courtesy David & Charles

Ex-LSWR 'T1' 0−4−4T No.3. This engine was among a group of 'T1s' allocated to the SDJR during World War II to work the Bridgwater, Wells and Burnham branches. *HMRS Collection*

JULY–SEPTEMBER 1939 TIMETABLE

	am	am	am	pm	pm	pm	pm	pm
Bridgwater	8.05	9.50	11.30	1.10	2.55	5.10	6.30	9.00
Bawdrip Halt	8.10	9.55	11.35	1.15	3.00	5.15	6.35	9.05
Cossington	8.14	9.59	11.39	1.19	3.04	5.19	6.39	9.09
Edington Jn	8.21	10.06	11.46	1.26	3.11	5.26	6.46	9.16

	am	am	am	pm	pm	pm	pm	pm
Edington Jn	7.38	8.30	11.00	1.35	4.35	5.35	7.15	9.25
Cossington	A	8.36	11.07	1.41	4.41	5.41	7.21	9.31
Bawdrip Halt		8.40	11.11	1.45	4.45	5.45	7.25	9.35
Bridgwater	7.53	8.41	11.17	1.53	4.53	5.52	7.33	9.41

A = Stops to set down passengers on request.

MAY 1945 TIMETABLE

	am	pm	pm	pm
Bridgwater	9.45	1.20	2.35	6.35
Bawdrip Halt	9.50	1.25	2.40	6.40
Cossington	9.55	1.30	2.45	6.45
Edington Jn	10.07	1.42	2.57	6.57

	am	am	pm	pm	pm
Edington Jn	8.50	11.00	1.50	3.15	7.10
Cossington	8.55	11.05	1.55	3.20	7.15
Bawdrip Halt	9.00	11.10	2.00	3.25	7.20
Bridgwater	9.12	11.22	2.12	3.37	7.32

By 1947 the service had been increased to five down and six up trains and the journey time reduced to 18 minutes. This appears to have been the normal scheduled time for the rest of the Bridgwater Railway's life, there being few significant differences in 1948 and 1951. It is a little sad to think the passenger timings of 1951 only matched the goods timing of 1892.

JUNE–OCTOBER 1947 TIMETABLE

	am	am	pm	pm	pm			
Bridgwater	9.40	10.45	2.10	4.00	6.40			
Bawdrip Halt	9.47	10.50	2.15	4.05	6.45			
Cossington	9.52	10.55	2.20	4.10	6.50			
Edington Jn	10.00	11.03	2.28	4.18	6.58			

					SX	SO		
	am	am	am	pm	pm	pm	pm
Edington Jn	8.22	10.10	11.15	2.40	5.15	5.40	7.20
Cossington	8.30	10.15	11.20	2.50	5.22	5.45	7.25
Bawdrip Halt	8.35	10.20	11.25	2.55	5.27	5.50	7.30
Bridgwater	8.45	10.28	11.33	3.05	5.35	5.58	7.38

SX = Saturdays excepted
SO = Saturdays only

1948 TIMETABLE

DOWN		Pass.	Pass.	Pass.	Mixed	Pass.	Goods
		am	am	pm	pm	pm	pm
Bridgwater	dep.	9.42	10.38	1.40	3.35	6.30	8.15
Bawdrip Halt	arr.	9.48	10.44	1.46	4.01	6.36	
	dep.	9.49	10.45	1.47	4.02	6.37	
Cossington	arr.	9.53	10.49	1.51	4.06	6.41	
	dep.	9.54	10.50	1.52	4.07	6.42	
Edington Jn	arr.	10.00	10.56	1.58	4.13	6.48	8.37

UP		Mixed	Pass.	Pass.	Mixed	Pass.	Pass.
		am	am	am	pm	pm	pm
Edington Jn	dep.	8.26	10.10	11.15	2.30	5.28	7.25
Cossington	arr.	8.33	10.16	11.11	2.36	5.34	7.31
	dep.	8.34	10.17	11.12	2.43	5.35	7.32
Bawdrip Halt	arr.	8.39	10.21	11.16	2.47	5.39	7.36
	dep.	8.40	10.22	11.17	2.48	5.40	7.37
Bridgwater	arr.	8.48	10.28	11.23	2.55	5.46	7.43

SEPTEMBER 1951 TIMETABLE

	am	am	pm	pm	pm	
Bridgwater N.	9.40	10.35	1.40	3.55	6.30	
Bawdrip Halt	9.47	10.43	1.45	4.00	6.35	
Cossington	9.52	10.48	1.50	4.05	6.40	
Edington Jn	10.00	10.56	1.58	4.13	6.48	

	am	am	am	pm	pm	pm
Edington Jn	8.25	10.10	11.05	2.35	5.35	7.25
Bawdrip Halt	8.30	10.15	11.10	2.48	5.40	7.30
Cossington	8.38	10.20	11.15	2.53	5.45	7.35
Bridgwater	8.48	10.28	11.23	3.03	5.53	7.43

Bearing in mind how little the Bridgwater line was used and how economies were being sought in its operations for most of its existence, it is hardly surprising that its closure came early. The day of the last passenger train, 29th November, 1952, was a sad occasion. As on the opening day it poured with rain. Driver Charlie King and Fireman George Brooks departed with the 7.30 pm from Edington for Bridgwater. Their Johnson 0−4−4T hauled a solitary coach. Unlike the well-attended closures of lines in the Beeching era (in the 1960s), there were only six passengers on board. One of these, David St John Thomas, wrote in his *Regional History of the Railways of Great Britain, Vol.1*, that the 'passengers were a handful of railway enthusiasts and one or two reporters'. Will Locke was one of the few passengers. He described it as a sad occasion, not only because he had been a company servant but also because he remembered trips by train to picnic in the Poldens when he was a boy. The last passenger train was witnessed by at least two people who had seen the first train in 1890; Mr B. Jeans of Bridgwater and Mr Arthur Cox of Burtle who recalled many trips on the line and especially the crowded trains on market days and at the time of the Bridgwater Fair and Carnival.

Will Locke was on duty when the last goods train ran. He and signalman Dennis Ashill were the only ones to see it leave for the last time on 1st October, 1954.

Chapter Eleven
Conclusion

The Bridgwater Railway was just one of hundreds of small branch lines which by themselves could never be commercially viable. As part of a larger system however, they had a value that could not be explained sufficiently in monetary terms.

Although I would hesitate to call the Bridgwater branch typical, it did share many factors with other branches. Its promotion and building were relatively late and this alone is indicative of its likely profitability and early candidacy for closure. The poverty of the Somerset & Dorset Railway, the rivalry between the S&D and the B&ER, discontent with the latter's monopoly in Bridgwater, were all essential factors in the promotion of the line, but it took the catalysing force of the profit motive liberally lubricated with deceit, deviousness and greed to produce the Bridgwater Railway. This was mostly done in the melting pot of Westminster and its environs where were clustered together the offices of solicitors, engineers, contractors and financiers whose intrigue, plot and counter-plot made a lucrative business of railway lines that became millstones to their operators.

The scandal of bribery, inordinate parliamentary expenses, camouflaged usury and excessive profit margins were not peculiar to the Bridgwater Railway. If the Bridgwater Railway was a product of this bed of corruption, so were scores of other lines. The pressure of time limits, penalty clauses and shortage of willing capital forced desperate schemes into the hands of the ruthless. One feels sympathy for those honest individuals who promoted railways for the good of their locality and found themselves having to deal with unscrupulous men.

Once it was built, the Bridgwater Railway rendered a service to its community in the form of local employer, carrier and provider of a social network. It was capable of rising to occasions of importance when circumstances (such as wartime or the Fair) brought larger traffic, but these were exceptions to a generally limited potential from a rural community in which the major centre of population and trade was already connected by rail. Two world wars and an intervening depression took their toll on the nation's railways, and, with the development of road transport (in which carriers did not have to bear the full costs of the permanent way), it was inevitable that identifiable areas of non-profitability should be eliminated. Small country branch-lines were prime candidates for the accountants' attention.

The Bridgwater line was such a loss maker that it did not even survive long enough for Dr Beeching's axe. It is a depressing thought that much of our railway system was built and destroyed by the profit motive. Of course one could equally well argue that this is part of a natural course of events which dictates the innovation of a system when it is needed and ensures its decline when the need recedes. Also, the very factors which ended branch lines heightened the public interest in railways. The acquisition of old station buildings and signal boxes for living accommodation, the sizeable market for railway magazines and books, the market in railway memorabilia and the passions aroused by the preservation movement: these are all evidence of a high regard and affection in the public mind for a transient transport system that evoked a multitude of priceless experiences and emotions.

SDJR railwaymen at Edington Junction: *left* to *right* porter Ivor Meader, fireman Sid Puddy, driver Frank Braund and guard Jim Turner J.P. *SDRT Archive*

Will Locke during his days as a railwayman on Cossington station. *SDRT Archive*

Chapter Twelve

Reminiscences of the Bridgwater Railway

by Will Locke

My earliest recollection of the Somerset & Dorset Railway at Bridgwater was about 1923 when, with about 150 Sunday School members and parents, we assembled at the terminus to await the arrival of an 8-coach train to Burnham-on-Sea. It was also a nostalgic memory that in the 1920s my mother took me during school holidays to Cossington station and thence to picnic on the Polden Hills. It was often a 3-coach set with a parcel van. One could hear the familiar sound of milk churns being loaded while a fair number of passengers entrained. In this rural area folk found the service very convenient for shopping in Bridgwater.

Since this early baptism it was my ambition to join the S&DJ although many years passed before this was possible, because in pre-war days it was difficult to obtain employment on the railway as it was thought to be a good situation. It was so often the case of having relatives on the railway to recommend you for a job. When at last I became a railwayman my first rule book was the Southern Railway's one in my working department, then transferring to the LMS (S&D) goods department as a checker, and finally the Western Region passenger department as station relief.

Bridgwater station was different from any other on the S&D system. It was a fair size brick building which included an entrance hall with booking office, station master's office, parcel office and also a ladies' cloakroom, and a lengthy island platform. The surrounding area included a timber yard and brickyards with the main Bristol Road running parallel to the line. The goods shed had two loading bay entrances and could accommodate six box wagons, there being a small crane on the loading platform and also a goods checker's office. Just outside the shed was a gas-lit goods office with a staff of five including the chief goods clerk. There were several small buildings such as the weighbridge and huts used for goods equipment, and an old coach used as a mess-room by brickyard employees, as three different brickyards were continually loading bricks and tiles in containers. This was a good source of revenue for the railway.

There was a story that the signalmen thought they should be on a higher grade, so an arrangement was made with the foreman of the brickyard to send double the normal amount of clay in trolleys across the line near the signal box on the day that the inspector was to investigate the case. He was amazed at all the work done by the signalmen, and as a result the box was upgraded to the delight of those concerned.

One entered the approaches to Bridgwater on an embankment leading to the bridge over the Bristol Road. There was a very high distant signal and there were two small sidings leading to Board's cement works, thence to a crossing gate over a road leading to Colthurst and Symonds Brickworks. In the centre of this road was a small tramway which was used to convey clay on trolleys. The signal box was just inside the gates opposite the permanent way ganger's house. The line continued to the arrival platform. A shunting operation was then needed to the crossover, and then the engine, after being uncoupled came back again to the main line. The signalman then set his road for the engine to come on to the coaches and propel them back to the departure platform. Here there was a loading ramp for vehicles and farm implements which were conveyed on low loaders or bogie-bolster wagons. The line running parallel to the departure platform was used by the Co-op coal depot. The next line was used for brick and tile container traffic. The remaining sidings were used to accommodate open and box wagons with general merchandise.

Beside the retaining wall of the cattle pen was a siding which was occasionally used for bulk timber loading with a manually operated crane. The cattle pen siding fell into disuse in later days, but on rare occasions up to 1946 it was used for transfer of cattle, there being a ramp leading from the road to the pens. This siding then continued over a road leading to a corn merchant and to two sidings at the rear of a saw mill. The sidings were used very frequently by open trucks loaded with timber. The goods porter was very active there tying tarpaulins on the trucks. There were stop blocks there but in earlier days the sidings continued to the wharf. I was told by one old guard that often as many as 45 wagons were shunted out of the wharf sidings. A wharfmaster had a large house which still stands today. The timber of this river wharf can still be seen but is now in a state of decay.

The earliest station master that older staff spoke of was station master Hawkins, an efficient railwayman and disciplinarian. I recall Mr Oliver who in 1912 was a junior clerk, but after years on the S&D system came back as station master. He was a jolly and friendly man whom I was proud to serve under. The last station master was Mr Beighton who transferred from Blackburn. He was a very smart man who was always anxious to keep up a good standard. He eventually went to Wembley. Mr Ball, the Western Region station master then supervised Bridgwater North until closure.

In the early days the chief clerk was Mr Whitehead. He was succeeded by Cecil Neil whose home was in Glastonbury and who did over 50 years service. Joyce Fear, whose father worked on the permanent way at Edington, gave over 40 years of loyal service as a goods invoice clerk. The foreman Fred Gilbert, whose service commenced as a junior porter at Cossington, completed 50 years service with the S&D and Western Region. Gilbert Ashill was a well-known personality. He was a carter, a goods checker, lorry driver and later a cranesman. Horace Pople can no doubt be remembered by many Bridgwater people as a tall, smart and very obliging railwayman. Of the signalmen Reg Seviour was well known also as organiser of the Allotment Association, Flower Show and Band Contest in Bridgwater. Reg Carter who worked on the main line at Shepton Mallett and came to Bridgwater in the 1930s and George Peperall who was at Cossington and for many years worked the Bridgwater S&D signal box almost up to closure, both ended their working days on the main line at Meads Crossing Box (Western Region).

Frank Braund was an engine driver up to the 1920s. He commenced his service in the 1870s on the Wells branch. He was a really dedicated driver. He told me that once when the train was delayed at Edington Junction he had to make up time. He did the journey in 14 minutes, which bearing in mind the climb to Cossington as well as the stop there was a really good achievement. The later engine crew were driver George Yard and fireman Norman Cook, two very dependable railwaymen whose timekeeping on this branch was excellent. The permanent way team of seven were mostly long serving railmen such as ganger Arthur Parson and subganger Bill Reakes. What a pride Bill Reakes had in his job! He specialised in trimming, to give the track a straight appearance. Other permanent way men included length-men Wilf Kent, George Adams, Ted Gore and Patrolman Walter Clarke. The permanent way was kept to a very high standard. The embankments and cuttings were tidy. When one looked over a bridge after new ballast had been laid one felt that here was the pride of the permanent way gang.

The goods checker George Parsons came from Shepton Mallet S&D and completed 50 years service. His father also completed 50 years on the S&D as a goods porter. Percy Jubin whose mother was a shareholder of the old Midland Railway spent many years at Bridgwater after being at Clifton Down. Victor Baker who worked on the passenger station and later as a driver was another long serving railman as also was a driver of an articulated lorry, William Lush, who came from Bailey Gate. Ed Napper was a well known carter with several brothers working on the S&D. Ed kept his horses beautifully groomed.

Bawdrip Halt consisted of a short prefabricated platform accommodating four coaches. This was built through the effort of the vicar of Bawdrip, who petitioned the railway company. There was a small shelter with seats. The guard on the first train during the winter months lit the two lamps and the guard on the last train put them out.

Immediately after leaving Bawdrip there was a deep cutting leading to Cossington. Cossington station situated almost on the summit of the Pol-dens, was blessed with wonderful views of the moors. One could see the smoke of branch line trains leaving Bason Bridge on the Burnham Branch and hear the engines climbing the gradient at least 8 minutes before arriving at Cossington. Cossington station served all the Chilton Polden area and up to 1920 had a station master with a staff of three porters. Fred Gilbert went there as a junior porter. In the 1930s George Pepperall and his wife lived in the station house. George later worked in the Bridgwater signal box. During World War II and just after, Mrs Pepperall was the leading porter at Cossington. Jeff Smith was porter there when the station closed.

In the small yard at Cossington was a cattle pen. The long siding was used for hay loading and general merchandise. The siding was also used by a Chilton Polden village coal merchant. The station building was of grey freestone. It included a booking hall, parcels office and waiting room with outside toilets. Adjoining the station was the station house. The fairly long platform could accommodate eight coaches. There was a canopy, but this was taken down after the war. On the platform was a ground frame which operated the home signals and the siding. As one left the station there was a deep cutting. On the Bridgwater side was a bridge. A short distance from the station towards Edington was Board's siding to a quarry that was used up to the early 1920s. It was the duty of the station staff at Cossington to be responsible for its shunting operation. During the war one of the Polden villages had a camp where blood was stored, so Cossington handled all this traffic.

The line from Cossington to Edington descended Chilton bank. Near a small river bridge the line passed a crossing keeper's cottage so isolated that it was lit by oil lamps and water was delivered there in 5 gallon cans dropped outside the house by the engine driver. The line continued across the moor until approaching Edington Junction there was another crossing keeper's cottage. This crossing was the responsibility of Mrs Rice. After the crossing one noticed a high distant signal. When the train arrived at the main line platform a porter shouted 'All change!'. The train was then shunted and set back into the Bridgwater bay. Often three engines could be seen in steam at this isolated moorland station.

Edington station included an island platform for trains to Burnham-on-Sea and a bay for the Bridgwater line departures. On the island platform was a canopy and a brick and wood building housing a waiting room, parcel office and booking office. On the north side of the main line was a lengthy platform for trains to Glastonbury, Evercreech and the rest of the SDJR system. There was a small waiting room on this platform. Nearby was the station master's house and the Railway Inn, now renamed the 'Tom Mogg' after the well-known signalman. Parallel to the Bridgwater bay was a lengthy siding used for general merchandise and outward loading of hay. This siding was used in later days as a coal siding.

Two well known signalmen at the busy Edington box were Harry Sweetland and Tom Mogg, who worked alternate weekly early and late duties. Tom Mogg's son Maurice was a guard on the branch for several years and is now an inspector at Crewe. The station masters I knew were Mr Beakes and Mr Pugh. Taff Rice was a porter while his wife was the crossing keeper. His son Roy also worked on the platform. Other porters were Ivor Meader and Percy Parsons.

Very often due to late arrival of the main line trains at Evercreech Junction, all branch trains were late, especially the Bridgwater train. At this isolated station the fire was kept in the waiting room as a very welcome amenity.

Three guards that I particularly remember were Charles Rousell, Harry Burge and latterly Jack Alford. Charles was most obliging and of a happy disposition. Harry was a likeable and dedicated railwayman whose home was in Bridgwater. He worked for many years on the Glastonbury–Wells branch before transferring to Bridgwater.

There were many excursions. One exceptional excursion took place about c.1910 when a great concourse of local folk were entraining to emigrate to Canada from the Bridgwater S&D terminus via Templecombe and Southampton. As a contrast to this scene I can remember in the days before closure when the passenger traffic had declined, the 10.35 am from Bridgwater comprised of one coach hauled by two engines!

The branch was noted for its courtesy. It was a well-known fact that when the trains had just left and passengers dashed on to the platform the driver and fireman would look back and then reverse to pick up the grateful passengers.

Some S&D men however could be awkward. A relief porter whose home was at Bridgwater occasionally had to do duty at Edington Junction over 50 years ago. After the last train to Glastonbury had been despatched it was the duty of the porter to close the crossing gates. One signalman would close these gates as a favour to let the porter catch his train back home. The other signalman refused, so the relief porter had to cycle home in all sorts of inclement weather, when just five minutes of shutting those gates would have saved a long cycle ride.

There were very few accidents during the 60 odd years of operation. Occasionally trucks would be derailed during fly shunting. I recall a case in 1947 after the last goods train had gone out. The breakdown gang from Highbridge was sent for (Mr Lawrence of Highbridge was the well-known carriage and wagon examiner who maintained wagons in Bridgwater S & D yard). By the time they were rerailed it was almost midnight. One wonders what country folk thought, as most could set their clocks by the trains.

I was told of another incident about a shunting operation at Cossington several decades ago when several cement wagons were shunted from the siding on to the branch. Before they could be braked they set off down the incline to Edington where they were diverted to the empty Bridgwater bay and crashed with formidable force into the stop blocks. Fortunately there was only minor damage.

There were amusing stories. In the early days a carter visited a local tavern on Christmas Eve, and after consuming more than the usual quantity, was lifted on to his cart while his faithful horse took him back to the goods yard. A goods porter came back after an excursion to a nearby inn to work with three others on a manually operated crane lifting bulk timber. This strenuous task was too much for our inebriated porter who was taken to the stables to recover out of the public eye. An elderly van driver whose allotment was near the station retold a story many times about the occasion when a travelling circus stabled the elephant van on a nearby siding. The resultant manure he spread on his garden, making his kidney beans climb to the top of a telegraph pole.

What a glorious heritage these S & D branch lines had. I have met elderly men who were proud to tell of their early days on the system and their family connections with the S & D. I am sure that in future days there will be many railway enthusiasts who will talk about this branch, and I sincerely hope this book will recreate nostalgic scenes that brought me so many happy memories. The day on which half a dozen folk, myself included, rode on the last passenger train, and the sight of the lights going out for the last time was a very sad occasion. Several years later I stood on the platform with relief signalman Dennis Ashill and saw the last goods train out. As it turned the corner past the crossing and out of sight I could have wept as so many memories came flooding into my mind. This dear old line had gone for ever.

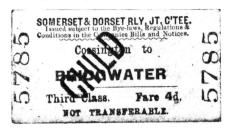

Bibliography

I have deliberately omitted footnotes, partly to keep down printing costs and also because I think they are a frustrating intrusion in a book aimed at pleasing before educating. The story is based on information culled from these sources:

At the Public Record Office:
Bridgwater Railway minutes, P.R.O. RAIL 68/1, 68/2, 68/3, 68/4, 68/5, 68/8.
Bristol & Exeter Railway minutes, P.R.O. RAIL 75/39, 75/47, 75/55, 75/72.
Somerset & Dorset Railway minutes, P.R.O. RAIL 627/2, 627/3.
Somerset & Dorset Joint Committee minutes, P.R.O. RAIL 626/3, 626/4, 626/5, 626/6, 626/10, 626/11, 626/16, 626/17, 626/18, 626/19, 626/20, 626/21, 626/22, 626/28, 626/29, 626/31.
Board of Trade Reports: MT/6-525/5, MT/6-697/6, MT/6-760/10, MT/6-882/4, MT/6-1114/2, MT/6-1399/6, MT/6-1449/4.
Somerset & Dorset Railway Working Timetable for 1892, P.R.O. RAIL 972.

At the Somerset & Dorset Railway Trust Museum:
Timetables for 1903, 1922, 1929, 1939, 1945, 1947.

At the House of Lords Record Office:
House of Commons Evidence: 1866 Vol.3; 1882 Vol.7; 1886 Vol.1.
House of Lords Evidence: 1882 Vol.3; 1886 Vol.2.

In Private Ownership:
Printed Parliamentary Evidence for 1875.

Published Work
Robin Atthill, *The Somerset & Dorset Railway* (David & Charles), 1967.
D.S. Barrie & C.R. Clinker, *The Somerset & Dorset Railway* (The Oakwood Press), 1978.
Robin Atthill, *Picture History of the Somerset & Dorset Railway*, (David & Charles).
Colin Maggs, *Highbridge in its Heyday*. (The Oakwood Press), 1973.
The Bulletin of the Somerset & Dorset Railway Trust, Nos. 40, 43, 51, 77, 78, 80, 94, 97, 113, 125, 126, 134, 137, 152.
D. Bradley & David Milton, *Somerset & Dorset Locomotive History* (David & Charles), 1973.
The Bridgwater Mercury 1952.
The Western Daily Press 1952.
Chris Hawkins & George Reeve, *L.M.S. Engine Sheds, Vol.4* (Wild Swan Publications), 1984.
Jack Simmons, *The Railway in Town and Country 1830–1914*, (David & Charles), 1986.
J.D. Harrison, *The Somerset & Dorset Railway in Public Archives*, (The Somerset & Dorset Railway Trust), 1988.
Reprint of *South Western and Midland Railway Companies' Somerset and Dorset Railway Joint Committee WORKING TIME BOOK from 4th October, 1920, and WORKING TIME BOOK, passenger and milk trains, from 14th September, 1931*, (Oxford Publishing Company).